THE AUTHOR

Robert Hume lives in Broadstairs, Kent. He has taught in several Kent secondary schools, and from 1988-2010 was Head of History at Clarendon House Grammar School in Ramsgate, where he managed the school football teams and ran the Scrabble Club. He has always enjoyed writing, and now writes features for the *Irish Examiner*. His books include a biography of Christopher Columbus; a G.C.S.E. History textbook; a historical novel (*Ruling Ambition*); an investigation into a Victorian railway disaster (*Death by Chance*); and five children's books – on Perkin Warbeck, Dr Joseph Bell, Olaudah Equiano, Mary Shelley and Thomas Crapper. Robert is currently a home tutor with East Kent Health Needs Education Service.

THE ILLUSTRATOR

Cheryl Ives was born in Walton-on-the-Naze, Essex, and trained at Bath Academy of Art in the mid sixties. She lives with her husband, Chris, just outside Canterbury in Kent. They have two daughters, Ivy and Natasha. After teaching for many years, Cheryl decided to retire in 2001 so that she could concentrate on portrait painting. She prefers to work in oils on canvas but also enjoys acrylic painting and pastels. Cheryl has illustrated each of the five books in this series, and uses family and friends as models for characters. She loves France and has conducted children's workshops in the Nord-Pas-de-Calais as part of a Beatrix Potter festival.

Robert Hume

Clearing the Bar
One Girl's Olympic Dream

Illustrated by
Cheryl Ives

First published in 2012

Stone Publishing House
17 Stone House
North Foreland Road
Broadstairs
Kent CT10 3NT

www.stonepublishinghouse.com

ISBN: 978-0-9549909-4-7

Typeset in 12pt Garamond by Troubador Publishing Ltd, Leicester, UK
Printed in Great Britain by TJ International, Padstow, Cornwall

'to promote equal opportunities, promote good community relations and eliminate discrimination relating to age, disability, gender, race, religion or belief and sexual orientation.'
(*Olympic Delivery Authority for London Olympics, 2012*)

Prologue

Herne Hill, south London, 30 June 1934, 3 p.m.

It is hot, one of the hottest days ever recorded. The athletes are warming up for their events – whether track or field. Arms and legs must be stretched, blood pumped faster to the muscles, breathing controlled. Just enough adrenalin must be flowing. Too little and they will never do their best; too much and they will be a bundle of nerves.

The British Amateur Athletics Association championships are under way. The sprinters pound up and down on the spot. The discus throwers flex their shoulder muscles. The high jumpers stand with their hands on their hips, rotating their abdominal muscles; then come the leg stretches.

But it's not all physical. Their attitude of mind must be right, too. They must have confidence, they must believe they can win.

Out of all the athletes present, Fräulein Gretel Bergmann is the only competitor from the Continent.

All the others are British, and represent the finest in their clubs all over the country, from Mitcham to Manchester. Nowadays, a foreign national would not be allowed to take part; but the rules were different then.

Having been cooped up in a stuffy train, and then squeezed with two other competitors and her father into the back of a taxi, Gretel now has to 'get the journey out of her legs.' She begins jogging, setting her pace just faster than walking speed, building up her pace but keeping well short of a sprint, just enough to raise her heart rate. By this time she is ready to begin her high jump drills – high skips, heel flicks and walking high knees. She keeps a really upright position, knowing that by staying tall she can clear the bar.

For many long months Gretel has been training, ready for this day. It is the most important event she has ever entered. She knows she can do it, clear the bar. She has to do it.

A flag is raised. She begins her run. Her left foot perfectly hits the mark for the last five steps. One – two – three – four – five and up, up and away. Her body instinctively does all the right things. Her right leg kicks up and over, her arms fly up. Her left leg swings over the bar. 'Careful, don't hit it with your heel,' she tells herself, and she is over. She knows that she has gone over cleanly.

Sitting there in the sawdust pit, the sun's rays burning into her long legs, Gretel sees the bar lying up there without as much as a quiver. She has done it – she has won the British championship.

But this is just the dress rehearsal for the main show. She can now dream of competing in the Olympics at home in Berlin in 1936, where the whole world will be watching her.

There is just one thing. She is not planning to compete as a member of the German team. Absolutely not. Gretel hates her native Germany. She will do everything she can to compete for Britain against Germany. For Gretel Bergmann is a Jew.

Chapter 1

Gretel was born on 12 April 1914 in the small town of Laupheim in southern Germany. All around lay open countryside, and from her bedroom window she could see trees, green meadows and far-away mountains.

For children the place was sheer heaven because the shopkeepers used to hand out biscuits, sweets and raisins to them. There were always delicious smells of food – the warm saltiness of bread baking and the rich aroma of coffee roasting. In the market place stood a drinking fountain where in summer she would eagerly cup her hands and gulp down the ice-cold water.

Gretel came from a prosperous Jewish family which some fifty years before had emigrated with other Jews from Bohemia to Laupheim. By the time Gretel was born there were about 300 Jews living in Laupheim, out of a population of 6,000; they took part in all aspects of town life and were represented on the council. The people of Laupheim got on well, Jews and non-Jews alike.

But Gretel's family were not strict Jews. As her father often pointed out, religion meant helping other people, not showing off at the synagogue: 'Be a decent human being,' he would say. 'That should be your religion.' The Bergmanns did not observe Jewish dietary laws, and only attended the synagogue for the festivals of Rosh Hashanah and Yom Kippur. Even then Gretel went under protest because she hated having to wear a hat.

Her parents, together with her uncle Marco and his children, owned a factory which made theatre props using hair imported from China. Bergmann and Co., as it was called, was her father's pride and joy, and was so successful that it shipped hair pieces all over the world. The factory employed 120 workers and had offices, a packing department, and stables that housed Bergmann & Co. horse-drawn carriages. Gretel never went into the factory itself; but when she played out the back at weekends the acrid stench of ammonia and bleach used to wash and dye the hair bit into her eyes and made them sting.

There were five of them altogether in her family – her father and mother; her brother Rudolph, two and a half years her senior; her younger brother Walter, born when she was twelve; and herself, a tall and skinny young girl.

Her father, Edwin, had a great sense of humour and loved playing practical jokes. It was too bad that she saw so little of him when she was a small child because he was away fighting for Germany in the First World War. Even when the War was over he was often abroad on business, usually in England, supplying wigs, toupees and false beards to the London theatres. So, those times when he was at home, puffing away on his cigar, were precious to the children who would insist on being played with whether he was in the mood for it or not.

She would never bother asking her mother because they did not get on. The obedient little daughter Paula Bergmann had hoped for in frilly dresses would turn into a tomboy who would rather climb a tree than do all the proper things expected of a dainty girl. She would frequently give vent to her disapproval with clicks of her tongue.

Paula Bergmann had been brought up in Frankfurt and always thought of life in sleepy Laupheim as a bit of a comedown compared with the bright lights of the city. Part of her problem was that she had nothing to do. She did not go out to work because women from her background didn't in those days, not paid work, at any rate – an aunt of Gretel's occasionally did voluntary work. At home all day long she was usually to be found in the living room, stretched out on the sofa with a wet cloth over her forehead, suffering from 'one of her headaches,' and getting the maid to fetch things for her.

The family had a full-time maid, a seventeen year old girl called Emily, who did the washing and ironing. She was helped out once a month, on washday, by two laundresses who spent the day in the basement boiling, scrubbing and rinsing huge piles of dirty linen and the children's mud-spattered clothes.

What fun Gretel had in that house – especially when her parents were out. The windows on the ground floor were so low, and Rudolph and she being as thin as matchsticks, they could easily climb in and jump out of them instead of using the front door. If either of them failed to land on their feet the other one quickly chipped in with an insult.

Inside the house, there were three floors and something interesting to do and explore on each. At the top of the house Edwin Bergmann had his workroom where he would mend anything that got broken, and make toys for the children.

Down a flight of stairs was the dining room which contained polished leather furniture and a plush carpet

An early jump

that tickled Gretel's knees as she played with their puppet theatre. At the far end a glass sliding door led into an amazing library, stacked from floor to ceiling with books on every imaginable subject. Sometimes she and Rudolph would sneak books from the library to their rooms on the floor below and read them under the bed clothes with a torch. At other times they would talk to one another down a piece of old hose pipe which they had managed to feed through a gap in the wall separating their bedrooms.

Just along the corridor Gretel would love to peer into the mysterious dark room where her father developed photos of the family. Although she hated having her photo taken, she was fascinated to watch the pictures taking shape as they lay in a tray of murky acid.

How Gretel loved that big house, which was so warm and cosy in winter because it was centrally heated. And how different it was from that of her friend Maja next door where the air was stale and stank of cheese, fish and sauerkraut. Not so the Bergmann house which in summertime, with its windows all flung open, was airy as well as spacious, and perfect for entertaining guests. On these occasions her parents would pack her and Rudolph upstairs. From behind the banisters, they would spy on guests, rushing back to their rooms when one of them came upstairs to go to the toilet.

Many visitors came to the house, including a particularly ugly-faced man who was a friend of their father's. One day, when the maid was carrying a tray full of glasses Rudolph ran across in front of her: 'Hey, Emily! Don't you think that man looks a bit like this?' He screwed up his face into an ape-like grimace. The poor girl doubled up with laughter and only just managed to set down her tray.

Rudolph also loved playing practical jokes on guests. Their piano teacher came weekly. This greedy little man, whose hair oozed grease, loved his cigars even more than her father did; and when he was offered one he would help himself to a fistful. So she and her brother filled the cigar box with beetles. When he reached for a cigar, the beetles swarmed all over him. The pair of them had trouble stifling their giggles, and she was sure that her father, too, only just managed to hide a smile.

As to other amusements, they had to make their own because the family had no radio, and television had not yet been invented. When she and Rudolph weren't teasing one another and rushing around the house, Gretel spent a lot of time in the garden playing with her friends Maja (the one whose house stank) and Wolfie (his family name was really Wolff) whose parents kept rifles in their house. Or she could be found in the back garden, walking on the stilts her parents had bought them. Rudolph was already so tall that he looked like a giant on his!

'Alright up there, Goliath?' she enquired with an exaggerated upward turn of her head.

'What's it to you, string bean!' he quickly retorted.

In the summer months she enjoyed spending time on her own, trampling barefoot across the fields, looking for a place to swim. She would drink milk straight from the cow, and pick cherries and unripe apples that gave her stomach ache. Often she would go on walks with the family dog, Treff, an elderly Irish setter with a gorgeous silky brown coat, who loved swimming as much as she did. It broke her heart when Treff was crushed under the wheel of a cart and had to be put to sleep.

Her parents tried to console her by buying her a bike; and after this there were no limits on where she could go and explore. This was the life for her, in the countryside, not like her relatives, all shut up in their city apartments. She liked being out and about in the fresh air of Laupheim where times were fun, uncomplicated, and where she felt free and happy.

At least, she did until life began to change for the people of Laupheim – and for all of Germany.

Chapter 2

During her early years Gretel was taught at home by a governess they nicknamed 'Boja.' It was all rather embarrassing because none of her friends had a governess, and she was such a loathsome old spinster, too! They hated going for walks with her, and if they got the chance she and Rudolph would run off on their own. And as if her moaning and nagging them all the while was not enough, she would drive them crazy when they got home by practising her scales on the piano over and over again.

At seven years old Gretel was sent to school. She hated school from the very first day, resenting her loss of freedom when she could be out in the countryside.

There were separate primary schools in Laupheim for Catholics, Protestants and Jews. Gretel was sent to a Jewish school which consisted of a single room piled with musty textbooks and where the air was hazy with chalk dust. There were only two pupils in the first class - a boy and Gretel – and the teacher was kind to them. But next year, when there were a lot more children in her class, she was taught by a maniac who would chase naughty pupils around the room brandishing his cane.

When she was ten years old she moved to the secondary school in Laupheim. She now had a uniform, including a cap with a shiny black peak; as she moved up the school, the colour of the cap changed. The school day was much longer: five hours of classes in the morning, a two hour lunch break (when she rushed back home to play football in the street), then another two or three hours in the afternoon. Of the fourteen pupils in her class, she was the only girl and the only Jew. But it did not matter in the slightest.

All the time she was at secondary school she only had a couple of half decent teachers, one of whom taught her to play a mouth organ. The rest were hopeless. Her language teacher arrived each Monday morning with baggy-eyes and a hangover. He would set an assignment and return to his desk, saying that he would be keeping an eye on them from a hole in his newspaper. Nobody believed him, of course, and instead took bets on how long it would be before they could hear him snore.

The science teacher was an enormous man, with fat

Science teacher

cheeks, and glasses which had really thick lenses. The sweat patches under his arms and the greasy food stains down his front made him a very sorry sight. An egg stain was still visible on his waistcoat a week after the original 'accident.' He was a creature of habit, and would always carry around with him a little black book containing the answers to the science problems. One day the class stole it: without it he was completely lost.

But whereas the science teacher was at least fun, in fact great fun, her maths teacher was downright cruel. He was the worst teacher that anyone could possibly have. Being a girl, she was spared, but any boy who stumbled over solving a problem could fall victim to him. He would race over and grab the boy's hair and shake him back and forth until he yowled.

How she yearned for the summer holidays when the days were long and she was free again to enjoy her sports.

Chapter 3

It was strange that Gretel was keen on sport because nobody in her immediate family was at all into it. Her interest began at seven or eight years old when she went skiing with her cousins on a small mountain near Laupheim. She enjoyed herself so much that each winter after this she would go ice-skating in the street, and would even go shopping on ice skates.

Luckily for her, the sports club in Laupheim offered a good range of sports, including swimming and tennis, and the gym was only a few minutes' walk from their house. But Gretel realised very early on that her long arms and legs (she took huge, size 11 shoes) were best suited not to gymnastics but to field events such as shot-putting and high jump.

By the time she was ten years old she had already won quite a few athletics competitions. She realized that she had a natural talent for athletics, and did not really have to work at it. Perhaps she could become a coach or a P.E. teacher.

Her interest was seen as a bit weird for a girl, and especially for a Jewish girl. To be sure, there were more opportunities in Germany during the mid-1920's for girls to follow less conventional paths, pursue a career, even become an M.P. in the Reichstag, the German parliament; but Jewish girls, as her mother never ceased to remind her with many clicks of her tongue, were still supposed to stay at home and learn to cook and sew, and eventually marry a doctor or a lawyer. They still had their own traditional sphere of life, and the men had theirs, just as they had their separate seats in the synagogue, the women upstairs and the men downstairs.

But Gretel had made up her mind that her future lay with sport, and she competed with such drive that she started to win everything in sight. Occasionally she wondered what it might feel like to lose, but she never knew because she always won. What great fun it was.

All the more disappointing that her teachers, instead of being supportive were very negative, and ridiculed her involvement with sports. How she despised them for this; they made her so angry. She would teach them a lesson of her own by putting the absolute minimum into her school work. This might mean she only achieved low grades. But what did she care?

Gretel lived for the school holidays, and the freedom she felt when she was out in the fresh country air. One bright morning during the Easter holidays, just before she was twelve years old, her brother Rudolph, a couple of her cousins, together with her friends Maja and Wolfie, decided to go for a bike ride to a neighbouring village. They built up quite a thirst and decided to wash down their bread and cheese lunch with some beer that Rudolph managed to buy at a local shop. The warmth of the sun had already put them in good spirits, and the beer made them all the merrier.

'Let's go over to your house, Wolfie,' suggested Maja, her blue eyes sparkling.

They had been to Wolfie's once before, and loved it. The place was more like a castle than a house, with a tower and a stream they called the moat. But what made the house really irresistible was the collection of weapons – some mounted on the walls, others displayed in cabinets. There were exciting looking guns and shining swords; and hidden away somewhere there was supposed to be a live grenade.

Wolfie thought about it. His parents were away on holiday and he had been told that under no circumstances was he to bring friends back to the house. If anything got broken there would be hell to pay. But what a great time they could have!

Wolfie raised his head: 'Yes, let's!' he said with a grin.

All he had to do was persuade their young wide-eyed maid to let them in. That would not be too difficult because it was her first job and she was a bit of a soft touch. They would just tell her they were thirsty.

Twisting a plait round her right index finger, the maid stood listening to the little gang whimpering in the doorway. In no time they had persuaded her to let them in, and she scuttled off towards the kitchen to fetch a tray of cold drinks.

Quickly they drained their glasses, and as soon as her back was turned were charging up the staircase towards the attic. Wolfie took a key from a jar, unlocked the display cabinet, and took out a rifle. As he brandished it in the air, his eyes were like flaming torches. Everyone cheered and whooped.

'Now for a bit of shooting!' he yelled. And the troop followed his tall frame out of the attic and on to the roof garden.

Directly below them in the stream twigs and matted leaves floated by.

Wolfie took aim and fired.

Suddenly the gun burst into life.

His friends took a step backwards.

No one had believed for a moment that it was loaded.

'Who's next?'

Maja stepped up, took aim and fired at what looked like a piece of moss.

She missed.

Next, Gretel's young cousin wanted a turn. Before she knew it he had seized the gun. It seemed almost as big as he was.

'I'll help you,' offered Gretel.

As he scowled at her, his long brown hair fell across his face. 'I want to do it myself,' and he swung round to load the rifle.

All of a sudden the gun went off with a terrific bang.

Her cousin gasped, dropped the gun and ran inside.

Maja and Wolfie roared with laughter.

But Gretel was annoyed with herself for letting him load it.

It was just as well that he had been pointing the gun down. Thank goodness no one had been hurt.

Or so they thought at first.

But after a few moments Gretel began to feel a stinging sensation in her right leg, just above the ankle.

Injury at Wolfie's

Looking down she saw, to her horror, a hole burnt into her laced boot.

A wave of cold fear swept through her.

Rudolph carried her into the house, laid her down on a sofa and began easing off her boot and her stocking.

The others stayed on the roof in a state of shock.

By this time the maid had appeared, rushing in and out of the room in a right old state, updating the others on Gretel's condition, and cursing herself for letting them in.

As Rudolph towered over his sister he could see that blood was starting to ooze from her wound.

Help was needed, but they were not sure whether they should ring a doctor or their parents. Rudolph made a frantic call to the operator who connected them with their home.

Her mother answered the phone. She sounded tired.

'Gretel's been shot in the leg!' said Rudolph.

Paula Bergmann, six months pregnant, froze with fear and it took her a few moments before she had the presence of mind to send a message to her husband, who borrowed a bike from one of his workers and rode at top speed from the factory over to Wolfie's house.

An ambulance was called and Gretel was taken to an orthopaedic surgeon in Ulm.

That summer's long jump competitions were only a few weeks away, and she knew that she would not be able to take part. Much worse, if the injury to her foot was serious, it would mean that she would have to rethink the career she had planned as a P.E. teacher or athletics coach. Would that bit of fun at Wolfie's put an end to her sporting prospects altogether?

Chapter 4

Xrays were taken, and there was a long wait before they were ready. Gretel dreaded the results. Eventually the doctor returned, and showed them where the bullet had hit the bone. Fortunately, not much major damage had been done, her high-button shoes having saved her from a more serious injury. A surgeon extracted the bullet and bandaged her leg; she was given a tetanus injection and allowed to go home that same night.

Paula and Edwin Bergmann telephoned Wolfie's parents who cut short their holiday and returned home. They were absolutely livid when they found out what had happened, or most of what had happened – for the gang had a secret pact to keep quiet about who had done the actual shooting. Wolfie had been expressly forbidden to bring friends back to the house, but had taken no notice. As a punishment he was not allowed to go out for a whole month. As for the maid who had let them in, she was sacked and had to return to live with her parents.

For a few days Gretel hobbled around the house, but she made a rapid recovery and was soon able to continue with her sports – which now included ice skating, skiing, football, athletics, field handball and dodgeball. But more than anything she loved the high jump.

As there was no training ground in Laupheim, she helped turn over an old potato field, created a run-up track and a pit, found a couple of poles and some old rope, and started practising her high jump there. Some of the neighbouring children came to watch, and a few asked whether they could have a go; before long she was not only practising herself but also coaching them.

* * *

That summer, 1926, baby Walter arrived. His birth gave cause for a double celebration. Not only did they have a new baby brother, they also got their governess Boja off their backs because she was redeployed as his nurse. Although born a few weeks prematurely, Walter turned out to be a healthy baby.

Instead it was her dear friend Wolfie who became ill. He had been complaining of pains and feeling tired for some time, and had become very thin. For a while he carried on as usual, going out with his friends again once his ban had been lifted. But he soon became so weak that he started to spend more and more of his time in bed. Their family doctor referred him to the hospital which made the shocking diagnosis that he had leukaemia, a form of blood cancer. At that time nothing could be done for this illness, it was thought of as incurable. It was all so hopeless.

The only friend Wolfie wanted to see now was Gretel. So almost every day after school she visited him for an hour or two. As she looked at his almost transparent skin and heard his sharp intakes of breath, a cold shudder crept up her spine. She tried her best to make him laugh by remembering the fun they had had together. But as he grew weaker he was not always in the mood.

Often he would be angry. He began to doubt whether he would ever be able to finish school and take his exams, let alone go out with girls and one day get married. Would he even be able to get back into school? His life had scarcely begun; but if the doctors were right, he would very soon be robbed of it. The thought of this made him so upset that he did not want to talk at all.

Gretel knew that he had not much longer to live.

Even so, his death a few days later, just two days before he was sixteen, came as a terrible shock to her. That someone not much older than she could die was just too hard to accept. She thought that only old people died. It seemed very wrong. It made her bitter.

Chapter 5

At fourteen years old, boys became even more important to her than sport, and she found herself madly in love with a twenty-four year-old called Fritz who seemed to feel the same about her. Gretel had met him at an athletics competition and they had quickly become good friends or, in her mother's words, yet another member of her 'sporting family.'

Fritz exuded charm and behaved like a real gentleman. He was a fully qualified architect and held a pilot's licence, which made him doubly glamorous. Her friends were so envious because all they had were their pimply-faced boyfriends who had no social graces whatsoever.

Despite her best efforts to keep him secret, her mother found out about him. No tongue clicks on this occasion. This time she hit the roof well and proper: 'What can you be thinking of?' 'He's almost twice your age! You are never, never, never to see that man again!'

Gretel simply ignored her; and even when Fritz was transferred to Berlin, they carried on writing to one another. Her mother intercepted his very first letter and made another terrible scene. So, from then onwards, Gretel got Fritz to send his letters to the brother of a friend. But the long-distance romance was not much fun, and after a while it fizzled out.

By then, Germany was beginning to be affected by what was happening in the U.S.A. On 'Black Thursday,' 24 October 1929, the value of shares on the New York stock market in Wall Street collapsed. The impact of this was felt everywhere but Germany was hit particularly badly. Money that the U.S.A. had invested in German companies was withdrawn by American banks over night. German businesses had to close and millions of people lost their jobs. Would the Bergmann family business be affected in some way, Gretel wondered? How could all this have happened? Many Germans blamed their government, and started to listen to a new party that promised to get the country out of this mess. Its name was the Nazi party.

* * *

Gretel's relationship with her parents seemed to get worse by the day, and there was one showdown after another. They had their idea how her life should proceed and she had her own plans. They wanted her to go to college, but she had discovered that at sixteen years old really good athletes could skip college and go directly from school to the University for Physical Education in Berlin. As Berlin was over four hundred miles away, this would mean leaving home; however, her parents thought that sixteen was too young to leave home, and since her father would be paying for her education, he was determined to have the final say. She would just have to put up with it; well, for the moment, at any rate.

To make matters worse, she would now miss the company of young men at school because in the following spring her parents enrolled her in an all-girls school in Ulm. This involved a daily commute of about fifteen miles each way, getting up at the crack of dawn to catch the train at 5.45 a.m. Classes did not end until 5 p.m., and if she stayed on for sports it meant missing the last train and having to walk home along a dark, scary country road.

Since she began spending so much of her time at Ulm it made sense to leave the Laupheim club and join the Ulm athletics club, known as the U.F.V. (Ulmer Fussball Verein). At first she felt like a traitor, but she soon shrugged off these feelings. After all, the U.F.V.

promised to send her on a training course with one of the best German coaches.

When the track season got under way in 1930 she competed all over southern Germany, and was sometimes entered in up to six different events – 100 metres, javelin, discus, shot, long jump and high jump. Often she won every event, accumulating lots of medals for the U.F.V., and the name of Gretel Bergmann appeared regularly in the sports pages of the Monday newspapers.

In 1931 she was ranked fourth in Germany for high jump, and with her jump of 4' 11" (1.50m) she was only three-quarters of an inch away from first place. Her parents slowly came to accept that she was who she was, and not who they wanted her to be. Her father started a scrapbook of press cuttings. Her mother managed a pained smile.

* * *

At about this time she met Rudi. He was twenty-five and worked in Ulm as a graphic artist. Although he shared her brother's name, in other ways he could not have been more different. Whereas Rudolph was dark, Rudi had blond hair. Whereas Rudolph was skinny and awkward, Rudi was broad-shouldered and confident, the most handsome man she had ever met. The thought that she was Jewish and he was not did not come into the picture, and in an instant she fell head over heels in love with him. 'Although I had imagined myself being in love with each of my previous boyfriends,' she said 'this was different, this was real.'

By this time Gretel was lodging in Ulm, and did not have to worry about catching the last train home. So they could meet every day after he had finished work for a cup of coffee in the plaza close to the cathedral before cycling to the stadium and having a meal.

When they kissed one another goodnight, all she could think about was them meeting again the following day. Gretel still had plans to study P.E. at the University of Berlin; but as soon as she had completed her course and Rudi had a good job, they would marry. And her mother could click her tongue as much as she liked about her marrying a non-Jew.

For a while she stopped concentrating on her sport, and in the high jump she slipped into fifth place. But did it bother her? Not one bit. Life had never been so beautiful and Gretel was very happy.

Chapter 6

On 30 January 1933, when Gretel was 18, the president of Germany, Paul von Hindenburg, appointed Adolf Hitler as Chancellor. 'At first this move did not have a particular impact on anyone's life,' she said. It was true that on the streets there were more soldiers in brown shirts (the so-called 'Storm Troopers' or Sturm Abteilung, S.A.); but most people she knew thought of them as thugs and loudmouths who were not there to stay. Certainly, it made no difference to her and Rudi, who continued to meet every evening at the plaza café in Ulm.

But before long the Nazis were everywhere – marching, singing, riding by in trucks, parading by torchlight. Their black helmets which came low down on their forehead, level with their eyebrows, made them look sinister.

Soon Gretel's neighbours were flocking to rallies to hear their new leader speak. Hitler would keep his audience spellbound with promises of a glittering future for Germany.

'The misery of our people is terrible!' he said. Millions of industrial workers were unemployed. Hitler promised jobs for men building motorways, schools and hospitals, jobs in the army, the air force and the weapons factories, and protection for businessmen against Communists.

Working women would have to quit their jobs because the place of women in Hitler's Germany was to produce babies, bring up children and care for their home and husband. Paula Bergmann was more than happy when she got to hear this: it was exactly what she had been telling her darling daughter for many years.

To acknowledge the importance of their role, mothers bearing lots of children would be awarded medals, just like in the Olympics: bronze for four children, silver for six, and a gold medal for eight. They were not to wear trousers like the modern German women, but conventional skirts. More agreement when Frau Bergmann heard this.

Plenty of people in Laupheim had got used to the free and easy 1920s and were against the changes; but they feared the consequences of complaining. At the very least they risked being humiliated in public; at

Hitler speaks

worst they faced losing their job, even being put into a concentration camp.

Provided you conformed to Hitler's ideas of a perfect race you had no cause to worry. It was these ideas that made Gretel's blood boil. Hitler claimed that the so-called Aryan race of healthy, slim, blond-haired and blue-eyed Germans was superior and would one day take over the world. This so-called 'master race' needed to protect itself from 'inferior' races – blacks, Gypsies, Slavs, and above all, Jews.

For Hitler, it was the Jews who were the lowest form of humanity. They were 'undesirables,' 'a germ, infecting society.' In the Nazi-controlled newspaper *Der Stürmer,* her neighbours in Ulm read how 'the Jews are our misfortune,' they were everywhere, they controlled everything, they had stolen to become rich, they were parasites, feeding off the countries in which they lived. They had lost Germany the War and so deserved to be punished.

Before long, to be a Jew in Germany was to suffer. Jews were not allowed in restaurants, cinemas, parks, swimming pools or clubs. Non-Jews were afraid to talk to Jews in the street for fear of being punished, and Gretel found that she was shunned. Only nineteen years old and she was shut off. The only way she could see her non-Jewish friends was if they came to the house at night and entered through the back door. Gretel was too shocked to express her feelings.

At least she had her sports, or so she thought.

But out of the blue, a few weeks later, she received a letter from her club, the U.F.V., informing her that her membership had been terminated and that she was no longer welcome. 'How was it possible that I had been declared a leper almost overnight?'
Arriving, as it did, around the time of her birthday the letter made a most unwelcome present.

Further bad news was to follow. The University of Berlin wrote to her, saying she could not enrol on her P.E. course 'until this whole thing blows over.' That surely did not stop her from entering competitions, but when she tried to do so she was told she was ineligible because she was not a member of the German Track and Field Association. But how could she become a member when no Jews were admitted?

Over the next few months, all she could do was continue practising and training on her own in the hope that things would improve. She certainly wasn't prepared to give up.

The situation was now desperate for the Jews of Laupheim. They had lost the friends they had grown up with; they had been banned from public places; and now they were starting to lose their jobs and their income. It was as though they were aliens in their own country. How could their fellow citizens treat them like this? And what would the Nazis think up next? Feeling more and more cut off from the rest of Laupheim, they turned in on themselves to find support. Perhaps if they kept quiet it really would all 'blow over.'

Chapter 7

However, when her brother Rudolph was forced to return from Berlin, Gretel wondered whether it really was just a passing phase. He had been working for the American film company Universal Pictures, but now that Hitler's racial policies were becoming clearer, the company had decided to pull out of Germany.

By this time her baby brother Walter was having problems too. He was six years old and had been at school for almost a year. Until now he had been used to having his friends round to play; but under the new laws Jewish children could no longer associate with Aryans. It was hard explaining to him how his classmates had suddenly become his enemies.

This was because in German schools children were taught to hate Jews. Routinely they were ordered out in front of the class to have their Jewish features pointed out. In the books Walter used, but which he was never allowed to take home, he said that Jews were shown as freaks – grotesquely fat, bow-legged and miserable.

In his history lessons, he was taught about lands with strange sounding names that had once been part of Germany and that must be recaptured. In science he learned about explosives; in maths he had to do sums about the number of Jews in Germany.

One day his teacher read the class the tale of the *Poisonous Mushroom* in which a mother is picking mushrooms with her son. There are good mushrooms and poisonous ones, she explains, just like there are good people and bad people – and the bad people are the Jews.

After school the older children went to clubs such as Hitler Youth and the League of German Maidens where they sang Nazi songs and listened to lectures. They were told about the superiority of the Aryan 'master race' and how they should never trust the inferior Jew. The next day they would pick on Walter more than ever. He was spat at, called names and shoved off the pavement. It got so bad that Gretel began to walk him to school. Still the spitting and name-calling continued; but she did not dare touch the children who were responsible, for fear of being reported. And she could not say anything because she no longer had the right to express her opinion. Anyone

A picture of Jews from Walter's school book

suspected of opposing Hitler's policies was an enemy of the state, and was likely to have their home searched, be taken away and imprisoned.

By this time it had become difficult for Rudi and Gretel to meet in public, so they decided to move from the plaza into the cathedral which they thought would be safer. But for a non-Jew and a Jew to be seen together, even in the cathedral, would have serious consequences for them. Someone who knew them – a neighbour or a maid – might betray them to gain favour with the Nazis.

The only thing to do was to start meeting in secret at night in the garden of one of Rudi's friends. They knew they were playing with fire. As painful as it was, they had to face up to the bitter truth: they would have to part.

And so one night they met for the last time. As Gretel recalled, looking back on her life many years later:

'We had fallen in love less than a year ago, dreaming of a happy future, a future now confined to the agonizingly short time left of this night. The pain was almost unbearable. The lifetime we had planned together would be over when morning came, and we devoted these few hours to expressing the deep love we had for each other. It was a night when the dark seemed to rush toward the dawn with alarming speed; and when the sky began to lighten we knew that reality, no matter how hurtful, no longer could be pushed away. We held each other in an embrace that we wanted to last for eternity. We cried. We kissed. We parted. We walked off in opposite directions, not daring to look back.'

Chapter 8

Autumn 1933. Hounded more than ever, some of the Jews of Laupheim were starting to think seriously about emigration. Trapped in a country where her own sporting prospects were now non-existent, Gretel understood their situation well.

For most Jews, emigration would involve a long nightmare of form-filling and waiting. In this respect Gretel was fortunate. Her father was able to use his work contacts in Britain, and that October she accompanied him on a business trip to England, where he was hoping to sell hair pieces to London theatres. But his main reason for going was to enrol her in a college to learn English and practise her sport.

Gretel's first impressions of England were not good: 'It had to be a toss-up what was worse, the terrible food or the equally miserable English climate. Rain, fog, cold, damp.'

While her father booked into a hotel, she stayed with the Gruenebaums, an elderly German couple who were used to taking lodgers in their spare room. Compared to her large and airy bedroom back in Laupheim, the room seemed tiny. A rather scary looking, coin-operated, gas heater helped take the chill off the dampness.

The furniture was sparse: Apart from the bed, there was only a battered wardrobe and an ancient chest of drawers with a mirror hanging from a nail above. On top of the drawers rested a white enamel jug which was filled each morning with hot water; once a week she was allowed a bath.

During the first few days in London she looked over some schools for gymnastics. But these were not for her, she was an athlete. However, the following week she and her father visited the London Polytechnic at its new site in Borough Road on the Thames south bank, and the principal, Dr Ingall, took them on a tour of the building.

When they reached the gym, she was thrilled to see that the high jump – of all things – was in progress. About a dozen girls were involved, some ready to jump, others performing their warm-up routines, stretching and skipping; the coach had obviously trained them well. But how strange it was to see an old-fashioned rope being used instead of a wooden crossbar; it reminded her of the old potato field back in Laupheim.

Noticing how her eyes shone, Dr Ingall asked whether she would like to join in, and without hesitation she said 'yes please!' Rope or crossbar, the high jump was still the high jump. It was easy enough to find her some gym kit but no shoes were big enough, so she had to take part in bare feet.

The rope was raised higher and higher, and each time she managed to clear it. Some of the girls gasped and cheered but some looked away as if to say 'who does she think she is?' Still, it was what the coach thought that really mattered, and after briefly conferring with Dr Ingall, Gretel was offered a place there and then on the London Polytechnic team.

With his real mission in England accomplished, her father shortly afterwards returned to Germany, while Gretel stayed on in London at the Gruenebaums whose kindness did something to overcome her homesickness. Perhaps she helped replace their daughter who had recently left home to get married.

Before long, Gretel actually grew to like London. She would spend hours browsing in the shops on Regent Street and sipping coffee in one of the fancy Lyon's corner houses, with their bright lights and smartly dressed waitresses. Although she had not been allowed to bring enough money to buy much or go anywhere, the Gruenebaums sometimes helped her out. Mr Gruenebaum had connections with the London Philharmonic Orchestra and sometimes got free tickets for a concert or an opera which he would pass on to her. One evening she went to hear the teenage violinist Yehudi Menuhin play.

The rest of her time she spent training in the Polytechnic gym or at its sports ground in Dulwich. The other girls seemed friendly enough towards her: they all had lunch together, laughed and joked non-stop; they told one another about their boyfriends. They were really fun to be with and helped her learn English. But although they went round one another's homes, they would never invite *her* home. Why? It had to be because she was a Jew. This really hurt. She had assumed that by going to England she would be leaving discrimination behind.

These thoughts had to be put aside because she needed to concentrate on her sport. All the while she had lived in Germany sports had simply been 'fun.' But after arriving in England, her attitude started to change. Now she wanted to do well; now she wanted to win; now she wanted to be noticed by the British sports world.

So, when the 1934 season began it came as a surprise and a disappointment that she faced such little competition. Even when she was given a handicap and made to start behind the others on the track, and had inches deducted in the high jump, she still kept winning. Her name started to appear in the daily newspapers. Gretel Bergmann was becoming famous.

Chapter 9

Saturday, 30 June 1934. It was hot at the British Amateur Athletics Association championships at Herne Hill, south London, very hot – said to be one of the hottest days ever. Edwin Bergmann, on another of his 'business trips' to England, had come to watch his daughter jump.

Having travelled by train and taxi, they hurried down an avenue flanked by pillars to reach the stadium, her father all the while puffing vigorously on his cigar. The arena had been constructed as a velodrome, and when they reached the top of the cycle track they were surrounded by young boys trying to sell them souvenir programmes.

They looked down on the running track, and the long jump and high jump pits in the centre of the arena. Gretel had trained hard for months to be in peak condition for this day. She knew she had to think positively, to really concentrate. She imagined herself flying over the bar, the bar being raised again and again. 'I can do it!' she told herself. 'No one is going to get the better of me!'

Her opponents had already changed and were out on the grass limbering up. Gretel was the only competitor from the Continent, all the others being British, and only one of these was known to her – Miss Milne (from Mitcham Athletics Club) who had won the championship the two previous years and was determined to make it three in a row. Gretel was even more determined to stop her.

A few minutes later she was out of the pavilion, changed and ready to join the others. Her warm-up stretches were going to be crucial. Blood must be circulating into every part of her body. Without them her muscles would be cold, and she risked serious injury.

Gretel had entered for the shot put as well as the high jump. But the start of the competition had for some reason been delayed, and now both events were scheduled to start at the same time, 3 p.m. The only thing she could do was forfeit the shot and focus on winning the high jump.

Straight away she got down to her jogging, building her pace up to raise her heart rate. Then came the drills – high skips, heel flicks, walking high knees. Always staying tall, keeping that upright position in order to clear the bar.

Three o'clock approached. The sun's rays seemed to beat down hotter than ever. She began to concentrate on her breathing: it would help her relax. And as she breathed out she could feel she was expelling tension from her body.

A voice through the loudspeaker announced the start of the event. The bar was set at 4'5" (1.35 m). Gretel sailed over with inches to spare. One by one, the other participants fell by the wayside. Only Miss Milne was left. Both of them jumped 4'10" (1.47 m), then 4'11" (1.50 m), then 5'0" (1.52 m). At 5'1" (1.55 m) they both missed their first attempt. They both also missed their second attempt. On their third and last attempt Milne missed. Gretel heaved a sigh of relief.

Everything was now in her own hands.

She tried to compose herself.

She paced back and forth, shaking her arms and legs to loosen her muscles.

She talked to herself, reminding herself of everything she had to do. She stared at the bar as if hypnotized, and told her body *this is it.*'

She began her run. Her left foot perfectly hit the mark for the last five steps. One – two – three – four – five and up, up and away. Her body instinctively did all the right things. Her right leg kicked up and over, her arms flew up. Her left leg swung over the bar.

'Careful, don't hit the bar with your heel,' and she was over. She knew that she had gone over cleanly.

Only when she was sitting in the sawdust pit and saw the bar lying up there without so much as a quiver did the real significance of what she had achieved sink in. She was thrilled. She had won gold. The British championship was hers.

Now she could dream of competing in the 1936 Olympics in Berlin. But not as a member of the German national team: No, Fräulein Gretel Bergmann would do everything she could to obtain British citizenship and compete for *Britain* against the perfect German 'superwoman,' with her rosy skin, golden plaits and shining blue eyes. She would say to the Nazis: 'Look, you bastards, this is what a Jew can do!'

Chapter 10

Surrounded by newspaper reporters and photographers, Gretel was presented with a solid gold pin, inscribed with a single word: 'champion.' She was stunned. It was by far the most beautiful winner's token that she had ever seen.

It took a while for everything to sink in. Then she could not stop grinning. Her father, never one to demonstrate his feelings, came across to her, beaming. They walked arm in arm over to reception so as to send a telegram home. 'We did it! We did it!' the message read.

Gretel took a shower and changed. When she emerged from the pavilion she was still grinning, and her father went across and gave her a rare hug.

'Well done, my dear!'

After more photos, they made their way out of the ground.

As they waited for a taxi to take them to the train station a man passed them carrying a newspaper, and they caught sight of big black headlines. Hitler had wiped out the S.A. whose growing numbers were a threat to his power; and their leader, Ernst Röhm, had been assassinated. Could this be the beginning of the end of the Nazis, she wondered. That had to be good news for every Jew in Germany.

Edwin Bergmann seemed less convinced, and by

British Championships, London, 1934

the time they got off the train his high spirits had long since evaporated.

'What on earth's the matter?' asked Gretel, as they left the station for his hotel.

He inhaled deeply on his cigar but said nothing, just stared at the early evening traffic with his dark, observing eyes.

'Your mood has changed.'

He smiled feebly. 'I didn't want to spoil your day.'

'For goodness sake what is it?'

'I've been told to bring you back to Germany,' he said, avoiding his daughter's eyes.

'Bring me back? Who's told you to bring me back?'

'Party officials. They want you back.'

Gretel was too astonished to reply.

Eventually her father filled the silence.

'The Nazis want to try you out for a place on the German team.'

They turned into the street where her father was staying.

'The *German* team? But I've been excluded from all sport. I am supposed to be *undesirable* and *inferior*.'

'They want you to represent Nazi Germany.'

'You mean in the Olympics?'

Edwin Bergmann looked down at the pavement: 'Yes.'

'Never!'

'That's what they say.'

She felt sick. 'I am *not* going back, do you hear me? Nobody can make me!'

'Gretel, just listen to what I have to say...'

She looked directly into her father's eyes: 'Is this really why you came today? To run an errand for Herr Hitler?'

'Why, of course not!'

For a while they just stood there outside the hotel.

Eventually her father continued: 'The International Olympic Committee might take the Games away from Germany if it is not seen to be changing its racial policies. The U.S.A. is threatening to pull out. Hitler is under pressure.'

'I don't believe it. They'll never pull out. It's all a stupid bluff!'

There was a tremor in his voice: 'You're probably right. But Hitler can't be sure. Particularly as far as the U.S.A. is concerned.'

'The U.S.A.? The U.S.A. never cares two hoots about what's going on in Europe.'

'It does this time. There are so many Jews living in the U.S.A. that their government has to listen to them.'

'So, the U.S.A. doesn't show up. That's only one country. There are dozens of others.'

'An Olympics without the U.S.A. would be unthinkable. It would have no value. They have some of the world's finest athletes.'

Gretel looked puzzled. 'So how does any of this concern me?'

'Hitler needs a star Jewish athlete to represent Germany,' he said softly. 'Someone to give the world the impression that Germany treats Jews well.'

'You mean *me*, don't you.'

Her father hung his head.

Gretel's heart sank. As she walked towards her lodgings her feet felt heavy. The bitter truth began to bite. As much as she hated the idea of returning to Germany, she knew that if she refused to go back, she would be placing her family in grave danger. But more than that. She would be putting other Jewish athletes at risk because they might be punished. She knew she had no choice. Return she must.

The next day she packed her bags and sailed home with her father. By returning it meant an end of all her efforts to become a member of the British Olympic team.

Chapter 11

Back in Laupheim, Gretel was thankful to be reunited with her brothers after so long apart. But Maja, her friend from next door, whose family were Catholics, gave her the cold shoulder. It was all most peculiar: They had been in and out of each others' houses since they were young children, and they had always been seen together. Maja was with her at Wolfie's on the day of the shooting. Suddenly it was as if she did not want to know her any longer.

Other things had also changed in Germany during the time she had been away. The man who had appointed Hitler, President Hindenburg, had died and Hitler had become president. He was now more powerful than ever, and Germans referred to him as the Führer. Everyone was 'encouraged' to attend parades and speeches, and hang out flags. When it was Hitler's birthday in April, schoolchildren were expected to place flowers around the Führer's portrait in class, just as if he were a god.

And what more adulation was in store for him and for Germany if he succeeded in producing a showcase Olympic Games in Berlin in 1936. Hitler wanted Gretel to be part of that success. He wanted her in his Olympic team.

Within a few months she was offered a place to train in Stuttgart where she was expected to study hard – not just practice but theory too: anatomy, physiology, hygiene and first aid. That was followed by a four-day Olympic training course in Hanover where she soon came to be known by the other athletes as 'Bergie.'

* * *

Early next year a letter arrived, calling upon her to 'represent my Germany, my Fatherland, in the most worthy manner possible.'

'My fatherland,' she muttered, 'the one that despises and persecutes its own people, and puts the fear of God into others?'

Gretel had been chosen to represent Germany. Her ambition had been to compete for England, *not* Germany. But could she turn down this opportunity to perform at the highest possible level? Dare she turn it down?

It was not long before she was invited to Ettlingen, the big German national training camp. One or two of the other girls teased her when they heard she had won the London championship (some calling her 'perfect Gretel') but there was nothing hateful and nothing racist in their remarks. Did they not know she was Jewish, she wondered? It seemed not. Or if they did they did not care. 'Bergie' was one of *them* – she ate with all the others, chatted and played ping-pong with them; and when the boys arrived they arranged parties, danced and drank punch together.

Her room-mate at the Ettlingen camp was a very nice girl called Dora Ratjen. All the rooms had bunk beds, and she had the bottom bunk and Gretel had the top. Dora was only eighteen, three years younger than Gretel, with thick bushy hair and a husky voice. She was really enthusiastic about her training, and every morning, while Gretel was still in bed, she got up, did some press-ups and went out for a run. It was clear that she was going to be a serious rival to her in the high jump.

Dora was a rather nervous girl and tended not to join in much with the others. She never showered with the rest of the girls, but went instead to a separate cubicle where there was a bath, and locked the door behind her.

In the changing room

Some of the girls made fun of her for this, and found her kind of weird. Poor Dora, thought Gretel, she was just shy, that's all.

Besides, Dora was quite different when she was alone with her room-mate in the evenings. She talked about her life back home where her parents owned a bar in Bremen. They showed each other photographs: In one of them Dora was dressed in the uniform of the League of German Maidens – a long blue skirt, khaki top and swastika armband. She looked good in it. On anyone else it would have made Gretel cringe.

Gretel's best friend at Ettlingen was Elfriede Kaun. With her blond hair and blue eyes she was the perfect specimen of Hitler's superior Aryan race, the master race. But what of it when they got on so well? They helped each other by discussing what they had done wrong on each jump, and how they could do better. As a result, their performances improved and they were excited at the prospect of soon competing for their country.

If only Gretel could get encouragement and advice from the coaches, who seemed more interested in training the other girls than her. They always managed to find excuses to shun her – they were 'too busy,' her performance was 'just fine,' they told her. She tried telling herself that this was because she needed less help than the other athletes did; but in her heart she knew that it was because she was a Jew.

Chapter 12

Her life was suddenly to change in June 1935 when she was won over by the broad smile and rugged good looks of one of her fellow athletes at Ulm. His name was Bruno Lambert, a medical student, and they quickly became friends. Bruno, who already had a girlfriend at that time, had entered the 100 metres and the long jump; but in spite of his height and strong build appeared to have very little talent at either. She did not know whether to feel sorry for him or to laugh.

Fortunately, Gretel continued to make great progress, and when she jumped 5' 3" (1.60m), she knew that she had equalled the German record. Once again, none of the officials came over to congratulate her. She could read their minds only too well: 'How could this inferior Jew have the impudence to put herself on the same level as the Aryan superwomen?'

Gretel's reaction was swift. In the past, doing well and trying to beat records had just been about winning an athletic contest; but now the prospect of beating the German women gave her a feeling of elation. The urge to lash out against the Nazis kept her going: She became like a madwoman, possessed.

That autumn and winter, as the days slipped by in a dingy twilight, the German government passed a series of laws which made the lives of Jews still more uncomfortable. These measures, which became known as the Nuremberg Laws, were intended to defend 'German blood and honour.' From that moment, Jews were forbidden to marry Aryans or to have sexual relations with them. They were classified as 'subjects' rather than citizens, and many rights were taken away from them. No longer could they take part in organised sport or belong to a sports club.

As a direct result, Gretel was forbidden to compete in the German Track and Field championships. The official reason given was that her Jewish sports club was not a member of the German Track and Field Association. So, technically, her exclusion was for her club's non-membership – not because she was a Jew.

Worse was to follow. In May 1936 Gretel was dismissed from her school in Ulm. It was a bitter blow because she only had another six months of her studies to go. Sickened and dejected, she returned to Laupheim.

By then she and Bruno Lambert had decided to meet again, and this time they had more time to get to know one another. He was also Jewish and came from Andernach in the Rhineland where his family was still living. Although he was only half way through his medical course he already had plans to become a general practitioner. Gretel liked this. She liked it very much, that and his attractive smile. How easy it was for them to talk to one another. And as they looked into one another's eyes they knew it was more than friendship. 'It was love at second sight!' said Gretel , looking back on her life. 'For the first time since I had lost Rudi, I knew that I could truly be happy again.'

Bruno continued to come to watch her jump, and as the Olympics approached more and more practice events were arranged so that the German athletes would be at their peak when they needed to perform for their country. After all, that was the reason why she had been asked to return from England. She continued to train hard, doing even more high skips, even more heel flicks.

And yet, one thing worried her. She could only come out of this whole business as a loser:

If, for any reason, she could not compete, she would be robbed of a lifelong dream to take part in such a fantastic event, an ambition nurtured by every athlete.

If she competed and lost, she and the rest of the Jewish world would be held up to ridicule by the Nazis: 'See, we told you, the Jew is inferior.'

If she competed and won – surely, a very good possibility – the consequences might be truly horrendous. After all, she would have embarrassed Adolf Hitler with the whole world as witness, and for that she would doubtless have to be punished. Just what would they do to her? Perhaps they would come and find her one night and break her legs. And what awful things might they do to her family? And to Bruno? She could not stop thinking about it. It was a living nightmare.

Chapter 13

On 29 June, just a month before the Olympics were due to begin, Gretel arrived with a few friends at the Adolf Hitler Stadium in Stuttgart to compete in an event. Unfortunately, Bruno had some college business and was not able to attend. As usual, she was the only Jewish athlete taking part; as usual, the officials spurred on the other competitors while giving her no encouragement; as usual, the crowd was hostile towards her.

But she was not going to let them rattle her. In fact, their attitude would have the reverse effect. Gretel Bergmann would put on the performance of a lifetime, one that they would never, ever, forget.

As the bar was raised again and again, she cleared it each time on the very first attempt. She was like a madwoman, determined to humiliate the officials, the spectators, and the entire Nazi party.

The bar was raised to 5'3" (1.60m), the German record which she had already equalled in practices. She gritted her teeth, ran up and jumped, clearing the bar with something to spare. Gretel Bergmann, an inferior Jew, had succeeded in equalling the German record. What's more, only three women in the world had ever jumped this high before.

Only a scattering of applause greeted her. None of the officials came over to congratulate her, and from the expression on the face of the man who awarded her the medal, he might have been sucking a lemon. Gretel was furious.

All that she could think about was the Olympics

Gretel equals German record at Stuttgart, 1936

in Berlin. They were now only a few weeks away, and very soon she would be called up.

Sure enough, a fortnight or so later a letter arrived, addressed to 'The Bergmann Family, parents of the high jumper.'

Rudolph waved the letter around teasingly in front of his sister's face.

'Come on, hand it over!'

'But it's not addressed to you, it's addressed to your parents!' he laughed.

'Give it to me!' She seized it from him and tore it open to get at the contents, a formal invitation to represent her country in Berlin. Gretel studied the letter intently.

Silence.

Her face grew pale.

Her breathing quickened.

The paper crackled when she turned it over, as if expecting to find something more on the other side.

Rudolph could sense the tension in his sister's body; it was like a tightly-wound spring. From the kitchen, Paula Bergmann stared at her daughter in silence.

Gretel looked as if she were about to really let rip.

When she tried to speak she found she could not. Her mouth was dry.

A letter arrives

Flinging the letter on the table, she rushed out of the room and thumped up the stairs. The door of her bedroom crashed shut.

Rudolph picked up the letter and started to read it:

'The Reichssportführer, who has selected the team for the Olympic Games, has not been able to include you in the team representing Germany during the period 1-9 August in the Olympic stadium. For each competition – except relay – only three competitors could be chosen. Due to your recent performances you yourself probably did not reckon on being selected.

But Dr von Halt [of the German Olympic Committee] is prepared to reward your willingness and hard work by offering you, free, standing tickets to the track and field week, including the Opening Ceremony, for the days 1-9 August.

Should you intend to make use of this offer please let us know. The tickets will be sent to you immediately. Unfortunately travel and living expenses cannot be included.

Heil Hitler!
Tschammer.'

The signature was an indecipherable scrawl.

Gretel just lay there on her bed, unable to move. None of it made any sense. She had been dropped from the German team because of her 'recent performances.' What on earth were they talking about? It was nonsense to say that she was not good enough, not of Olympic calibre! She was the joint German record holder! And she had achieved that record only two weeks ago. No, she was being excluded because she was Jewish. It was as simple as that.

If the Americans heard about this they would surely boycott Hitler's Olympics. But it was probably all too late because they were almost certainly already on their way to Berlin. How very convenient! So, her inclusion in the team had been a sham all along!

For Gretel, everything had suddenly changed. No longer would she have to fear what would happen to her if she won, or if she lost. No longer would she have to worry whether she was expected to raise her arm in the stadium and make the Hitler salute. It had taken less than a minute to read the words in the letter. But in that time all her hopes had been shattered. Due to an accident of birth, by having been born Jewish, she was being cast aside.

When she met Bruno there was little he could do to

console her. It signalled a cruel awakening from a beautiful dream, a dream of what might have been. The whole point of the Olympics was that athletes could compete regardless of their race, colour, class or beliefs. Gretel was angry. My goodness she was angry.

Yet, there was a tiny bit of her that felt relieved. A huge weight had been lifted from her shoulders. After all, what if she had won? At least now she did not have to worry about that awful possibility any more.

Chapter 14

Germany had been due to host the Olympic Games back in 1916 but they had been cancelled because of the First World War. Now, in August 1936, by hosting a successful Olympics in Berlin, Germany could show that it was a modern, well organized and (Gretel choked on the word) 'civilized' society. The Games would bring nations from all over the world together in a 'festival of beauty,' which it claimed would help to further world peace.

In the previous Olympics at Los Angeles in 1932, Germany had finished only eighth, and Hitler required a far better performance this time from the German team. By winning a clutch of medals the Germans would be able to demonstrate that of all the races taking part, the Aryan race was superior.

The German capital city was made ready. Hitler had decided that he wanted a completely new sports complex. His stadium would be massive – like nothing the world had ever seen before – and covered in stone or marble rather than boring old grey cement. It would hold 500,000 spectators and cost 20 million marks. Roads leading to it would have to be torn up and widened, and a new underground railway with a station called Olympia (just like in London) would be built.

A few months before the Games were due to start, Dr Goebbels's Ministry of Propaganda saw to it that all antisemitic signs were taken down from the streets. And there were plenty of them: 'Dogs and Jews not allowed;' 'Road closed to Jews, this is not the way to Palestine;' and 'The best Jew is a dead Jew.' All of them disappeared, as if by magic, overnight. Shop windows were cleaned: many had carried notices to say that Jews were not welcome. The glass showcases containing the antisemitic newspaper *Der Stürmer* disappeared from street corners, and foreign newspapers and political books all of a sudden became freely available. Convict labourers were taken off the roads and railway lines, and concentration camp inmates were taken out of the fields. All this, to give foreign visitors a good impression of Germany. And so completely fake. At times Gretel wanted to laugh. At other times she thought she was going to be sick.

Having consulted weather forecasts, the Nazis decided that the Games would run from 1-16 August so as to get the best of the warm weather. A tremendous campaign began to promote the Games. The organizers flew all over the world in a Lufthansa airline which carried on its fuselage the inscription 'XI. Olympiade 1936'. A stunt man flew over Chicago; while in London, men carrying Olympic placards paced up and down in the underground stations.

Meanwhile, at home in Germany there were travelling exhibitions of Olympic history. Gretel's neighbours went to watch the massive Olympic steel bell, nine feet in diameter and weighing more than twice the weight of two double decker buses, as it passed through Stuttgart on a ten day journey around the country.

An Olympic village, with its own gym, training track and field, swimming pool and sauna, shops and a cinema, was built in a lovely birch forest about ten miles from Berlin; but only to accommodate the men. Gretel's fellow women athletes would have to use tiny rooms in dormitories in the Reich Sports Academy. This was because the idea of female sports contradicted traditional Nazi ideas about the proper place of women in society. An S.A. leader had said as recently as 1933 that: 'we oppose women's sports... Women should remain womanly.'

But for an athlete to be a woman *and* a Jew, that was to commit a double offence.

Chapter 15

Opening day, Sunday 1 August, 1936. Television crews were in place in Berlin to film the Olympics; but the invention was new and the picture quality tended to be very faint and grainy. At 8 a.m. the Band of the Berlin Guards Regiment played in front of the hotel where the International Olympic Committee officials were staying. At 9.30 a.m. cars arrived to take the officials to church, while Berlin schoolchildren marched to the fields to take part in group gymnastics, obstacle races and synchronized club twirling.

The torch bearer arrived in Berlin. Carrying a torch was something new in the history of the Olympic Games – the brainwave of Hitler. The torch had been brought in stages by more than three thousand young men from Olympia in Greece, each athlete having carried it for a kilometre.

At 1 p.m. while the Olympic officials were having lunch with Hitler at the Royal Palace, the stadium gates opened and thousands of light-blue uniformed ushers showed spectators to their seats. The Olympic Symphony Orchestra played Wagner and Liszt as spectators sipped a special soft drink called 'Olympia.' Meanwhile, above the stadium an airship named the 'Hindenburg' flew an Olympic banner. By 3 p.m. one hundred and seventy buses had brought the male athletes in from the Olympic village. A million people, held back by thousands of Storm Troopers, stood twenty or thirty deep along the three mile route on which Hitler would soon be travelling in his open-top Mercedes. He began that journey at 3.18 p.m., exactly on schedule, when he left the Chancellory in a convoy of ten armoured cars. At 3.50 p.m. he arrived at the Reich Sports Field. Thirty-two minutes precisely, as planned.

'He is coming now. He is coming now,' announced the voice through the loud speakers. A great cheer went up. At 3.52 p.m., exactly on schedule again, Hitler walked through the Bell Tower, and entered the stadium by the Marathon Gate. He was flanked by seven uniformed guards and many plain clothes men. As he ascended the stone steps and passed the huge bowl which would hold the Olympic flame, mass hysteria broke out. Then down more stone steps to the very centre of the stadium where he had a grandstand view from a partly-shielded glass box. 3.58 p.m. The German national anthem was played. Drums thudded.

The gigantic bell in the tall bell tower, visible all over Berlin, began to toll for the opening of the Games. The flags of each competing country were raised, together with the Olympic flag with its distinctive five circles – blue, yellow, black, green and red.

The teams made their appearance. Athletes dressed in smart jackets and trousers began their march around the arena. But would they all give the Nazi salute? First came each nation's banner bearer, then the flag bearer, followed by the officials, women athletes and men athletes. The British team simply turned their heads towards the crowd, and were received with little more than a whisper. When the athletes from the U.S.A. marched by they placed their boater hats over their hearts, kept their eyes to the right and did not dip their flag. None of them gave the Nazi salute. They were greeted with catcalls. But the Austrians, Italians and French all flung out their arms to salute, and were applauded by the crowd. The New Zealanders mistook a German official for Hitler, and doffed their hats to him instead. Finally, the host German team marched by to rapturous applause, its flag bearer carrying a huge black swastika bordered in blood red, its athletes wearing white suits and yachting caps.

A recorded message from Pierre de Coubertin, the founder of the modern Olympics, was played over the loudspeakers. He said that the most important thing was to take part in the Games rather than to win. Few German people believed this. They had been drilled into thinking that winning was everything.

Suddenly there was a hush. Hitler was about to speak, but when he began he did so only very briefly: 'I announce as opened the Games of Berlin, celebrating the Eleventh Olympiad of the modern era.' There was a fanfare of trumpets and a twenty-one gun salute, after which the Hitler Youth opened cages and released 20,000 carrier pigeons (supposed to represent doves of peace) which had been brought to the stadium in a convoy of one hundred vans. They swarmed above the crowd, dropping little presents on the less fortunate. There was more music, this time by the German composer, Richard Strauss.

At 5.20 p.m. a blond-headed athlete – the last of the young men in the chain of athletes stretching from Olympia to Berlin – ran into the stadium, bearing the Olympic torch. Climbing a flight of steps, he went across and lit the burner. A flame quickly filled the huge bowl, and rose to three metres high.

Finally, the elderly marathon runner, Spiridon Louis, presented Hitler with an olive branch from Olympia.

The athletes swore the Olympic Oath, and

marched out of the stadium to the music of Handel's 'Hallelujah Chorus'.

The games were open. But Gretel Bergmann was not present.

Chapter 16

The first event was the discus. The women's discus was won by Germany with a new world record. Germany also took gold and silver in the women's javelin and men's hammer. The Olympics seemed to have got off to a very good start for the host country. But in the men's 100 metre sprint, both gold and silver medals were won by the U.S.A. with the gold being won by a black athlete, Jesse Owens.

Hitler watched events keenly, though not because he was interested in sport: apart from boxing, he detested it and was no good at anything. Some joked (in private, of course) that the only exercise he got was raising his right arm up and down. No, he was interested in the Olympics because he wanted to see the German medal tally rise and rise. Hitler's Games were designed to show the entire world that when it came to sport, nobody could do it better than the Nazis.

In the women's fencing competition, a very

accomplished German athlete with Jewish origins, Helene Mayer, lined up to compete. Unlike Gretel, she was classified under the Nuremberg Laws as a 'Mischling,' or someone of mixed blood, because only her father was Jewish. Although she had green eyes rather than blue, her blond hair was sufficient to make her 'Aryan' as far as the Nazis were concerned, and so she had been given permission to take part – the only German Jew to be allowed.

* * *

Despite the government's best attempts, it could not arrange the weather, which turned out to be cool and wet the whole of the first week. But the second Sunday, the day of the women's high jump, was warm, and it stayed dry.

The call to report to the women's high jump came over the loudspeaker. All the seats in the huge arena were filled. Everywhere there were black and brown Nazi uniforms, and blood-red flags with swastikas. All Gretel could do was imagine that she was there in the Olympic stadium.

In her days as an athlete, Gretel had lived one dream after another. Before Hitler came to power in 1933 she had been happy to imagine herself competing for

Germany. In those days she had some pride in her native country. Although a Jew, she had felt comfortable in German society. The other girls had been fun to be with and she had been accepted as part of a team. The thrill of winning had spurred her on to do something spectacular, to win gold, to beat a record.

That dream had quickly turned to dust under the Nazis who banned Jews from sports clubs. Forced to carry on her training in London, she began to dream instead of competing for England against the so-called Aryan superwoman. She planned to strike back against the Nazis and really rub Hitler's nose in the dirt. She could do no better than try to obtain British citizenship and compete on behalf of Germany's traditional enemy. What publicity this would attract, particularly if she were to win! Hundreds of photographers would be buzzing around her. There would also be radio, film crews and, no doubt, some of the new television cameras.

But that dream also came to nothing when she was told she must return to Germany, to be trained for the *German* Olympic team. A Jewish girl would be going to high jump for Hitler, and millions of people around the world were going to see her do it.

Gretel can imagine herself there. She deserves to be there. She wants to show what a Jewish girl can do.

Jews were being portrayed as the worst people in the whole world and she wanted to prove that this was a wicked lie. In her dream she is determined to succeed. She *has to* succeed.

The bar is raised to 5'3" (1.60m).

Only she and the English girl, Dorothy Odam, are still in the competition.

Both of them miss their first two jumps.

The crowd sighs.

Odam misses her third.

There is one big intake of breath.

It is now all down to Gretel.

She runs up…

… and clears the bar.

The crowd are on their feet applauding. Her father punches the air. Rudolph is jumping up and down.

She has won an Olympic gold medal.

Hitler is staring at her. His face is ashen, his expression steely. His eyes drip hatred.

There would surely now be consequences. The thud of boots up to her door at night, her family home being turned over, all their possessions seized. Her father might be taken away to a concentration camp, never to be seen again; they would receive one of those letters to say that, unfortunately, he had died from typhus.

Berlin Olympics, 1936

She has insulted Hitler. She has made a mockery of all his theories about the master race of Aryans. What would happen to her now?

Chapter 17

Reality was very different. Gretel Bergmann was not there. It was all just fantasy. Her fellow competitors had been told that 'Bergmann is injured,' but they were keeping her place open in case she recovered. And the girls believed it. So there were only two German competitors in the women's high jump: her room-mate Dora Ratjen and her friend Elfriede Kaun.

There was no T.V. in Laupheim. Nor was there a cinema where she might have watched the news. Gretel could have followed the Games in the newspapers; but she decided to blank the whole thing.

The bar was set at 4'7" (1.40m). The gigantic numbers 1 – 4 – 0 were placed at the ends of poles and inserted on to the huge score board, alongside the athletes' numbers and their attempts.

The competitors finished their final warm-ups and kicks, and took off their training suits.

The high jump began.

Ball for Canada was first and cleared the bar easily.

So did Carter for Australia.

And Dorothy Odam for England.

Now it was the turn of Elfriede Kaun.

Over she went too.

As did Dora Ratjen.

And Csák for Hungary.

At 5'1" (1 – 5 – 5m) Odam, Kaun and Csák all cleared again.

But not Dora Ratjen.

At 5'3" (1 – 6 – 0m) Elfriede Kaun failed at the first attempt.

But Odam cleared.

As did Csák.

Elfriede also failed at the second attempt.

Elfriede's third and last attempt.

She was over. The German spectators went wild.

With all three of them reaching 5'3" there would have to be a jump off.

At 5'4" (1.62m) Dorothy Odam and Elfriede Kaun failed.

But the Hungarian Csák cleared and won gold.

Odam was second and won silver.

Elfriede came third and won bronze.

Dora Ratjen was placed fourth and won nothing.

It was several days before Gretel could bring herself to read the results in a newspaper. How unfair this all was. Only two weeks earlier at Stuttgart she had cleared 5'3" (1.60m). Surely, she ought to have been in with a very real chance of receiving a gold medal.

Chapter 18

Gretel needed to rest and to think what she was going to do. She decided to take a complete break, a holiday in the lovely resort of Baden-Baden in the Black Forest, about sixty miles from her home in the south of Germany. This peaceful haven, situated in a gentle valley with a lake, hot springs and relaxing spa water, had been made famous by Queen Victoria and the German Chancellor, Otto von Bismarck, who had gone there for the benefit of their health. The composers Brahms and Berlioz had also visited; and writers, including Mary Shelley and Dostoevsky, had been there to think and relax.

Her time in Baden-Baden was spent completely alone, without talking to a soul. Nor, while she was there did she write a single letter to Bruno. Determined to keep a low profile, she had even made up a name for the hotel register.

Physically and mentally exhausted, she needed

time to regain her strength and think things through calmly. Every afternoon she would take a stroll along by the lake or take a walk in the gardens with their perfumed roses and towering rhododendrons.

Since the days when she used to practise jumping in the disused potato field in Laupheim she had come a long way. Then she was full of optimism, believing that anything was possible. But now she had experienced the real world, its unfairness, its cruelty.

After two weeks she had made up her mind. She told Bruno her plan – She had to get out of Germany. There was no future for her there.

Many Jews had emigrated immediately Hitler came to power in 1933, most of them hoping to return when things had 'blown over.' But emigration was harder now. Although most countries still accepted Jews they had also put strict limits on the number they were willing to admit. This was partly because the economic depression made them reluctant to accept immigrants who would worsen unemployment. But it was also because of antisemitism – though what country was going to admit this? Emigration right then was going to be difficult.

Her best bet was to try to emigrate to the U.S.A. After all, it was known as 'the land of the free,' where its citizens could express themselves without fear and where there was no discrimination or prejudice. Her brother, Rudolph, had managed to get a permit to work there, and had submitted his immigration papers soon after he was forced to move from Berlin. Gretel must do the same. Bruno would join her out there when he had completed his medical studies, and they would marry.

Before any of this could happen she would need to find a sponsor. Her father had an old school friend who some years previously had promised to help, so she asked him for his address and wrote to the friend.

It was a while before she heard from him, and when he did reply his answer was very disappointing. He explained how bad the economic depression was in the U.S.A. and that Gretel would have trouble finding a job. 'Maybe the situation in Germany will soon change for the better. Why don't you rethink?'

She pushed the letter aside in disbelief. Maybe he wasn't interested in helping her now that she wasn't famous after all? Far from being an Olympic star, she had not even taken part in the Olympics. She felt sick. It seemed that yet another door was being slammed in her face.

Chapter 19

Next day, her father wrote back an angry letter, making it clear how the situation in Germany, far from being likely to change for the better, was actually getting worse by the minute, and that Gretel needed his help to make a fresh start. Ahead of her she had a promising career as a high jumper, and in the U.S.A. she could flourish.

The letter worked, and the friend agreed to help, sending her the necessary paperwork which she took to the U.S. embassy straight away. The officials there showed great sympathy towards how she had been treated, and promised to deal with her application quickly.

Towards the end of January 1937, Rudolph prepared to leave Germany for the U.S.A. His packing had to be supervised to make sure that he did not take anything out of the country to which he was not entitled, and to check that he paid all his taxes. The job was entrusted to one of their father's former employees who had left his job to become a Nazi official. The arrival of this man at their house, with his eager, long-nosed face and full Nazi uniform scared them. He seemed determined to make the whole business as slow and unpleasant as possible, and they felt very uncomfortable under his intense scrutiny.

The following month, Gretel's visa came through, and she booked her passage to New York. It had not been an easy decision to leave her homeland, possibly forever – a land in which she had once been happy and safe. But she had been forced to leave it for an unknown world where she had no idea what would await her. And then there was her family – her mother and father, and Walter. Would she ever see them again?

Before setting off on that voyage she and Bruno visited both sets of parents to break the news of their intentions. In Laupheim her father was overjoyed, and slapped them both on the back; Paula Bergmann, with arms folded, gave them her blessing. Then they went to Bruno's home town of Andernach where his parents, brother and sister were delighted to hear the news.

Two days later Bruno and Gretel parted. She would wait for him in the U.S.A. where they would begin a new life together as man and wife.

Her packing was also supervised by the Nazis, but this time the official was a kind man with a face that immediately put people at ease. He sat with them, talking and even accepted a beer, while Paula Bergmann raced around, checking that her daughter had sufficient clothes.

On 9 May 1937 her family travelled with her by car to Ulm railway station where she would say goodbye and take the train to Hamburg. From there she would board ship for New York. Walter, who was only eleven, was crying his heart out. Only recently Rudolph had left; now his big sister was going, too. 'I can't stand it any more!' he cried. 'Everyone I love is leaving!' The last look at her family, maybe forever, was blurred through eyes filled with tears. It was a sadness mixed with anger against a system that was forcing her to leave purely for the 'crime' of having been born Jewish. As the train pulled out of the station, she made a solemn vow never to set foot on German soil again.

She must cling on to the future – a life with Bruno. It would be some time before he could join her in the U.S.A. The Nazis would not allow him, a Jew, to take his final exams at medical school, without which he would not be a licensed physician. And it was no use him accompanying Gretel to the U.S.A. because the

90

American Medical Association would not acknowledge his years spent studying in Germany, so he would have to start the course all over again. The only thing he could do was to travel to Switzerland and complete his studies there.

On 10 May in Hamburg Gretel boarded the SS *Washington*, the ship that would take her to New York. All she had was the maximum sum the Nazis would let any emigrant take with them – a paltry $4. She reached her cabin and opened the door. On the table was a bouquet of twelve red roses with the message: 'For you.'

Chapter 20

The Atlantic crossing was calm and not once did she feel seasick. The ship was crowded with passengers and it was exciting to be on board. Exciting, that is, as long as you did not think back to the ones you were leaving behind.

There was plenty to do in order to pass the time: deck tennis, ping-pong and physical exercises. She quickly struck up friendships with her cabin-mate and the other passengers, many of whom were also sailing to the U.S.A. to escape oppression and begin a new life where they would no longer live in fear.

After ten days they sailed past the Statue of Liberty and into New York harbour.

Before she was permitted to disembark, Gretel had to have her papers scrutinized. There was a long wait. She began to worry that something might not be quite in order, that she would be detained on Ellis Island. Fortunately all her papers were found to be in perfect order and at last she was allowed down the gangplank.

Arrival in New York

On the quay was Rudolph, as skinny as ever, all six feet three inches of him, jumping up and down and waving a small American flag.

'So how come it took you so long? Couldn't tear yourself away from some good-looking steward?'

'You sure didn't get any better-looking since I saw you last.'

'What the hell is all this stuff you're bringing along? I'm getting a hernia just looking at it.'

'Yeah, you never did have any muscles, you weakling!'

They laughed and hugged one another. It seemed as if nothing had changed.

Rudolph pointed to one of the customs officials: '*He's* lenient with Jewish refugees.' So she made a beeline for him. Sure enough, he opened her suitcase, quickly shut it again and waved her through.

In less than an hour after coming ashore, they were in the back of a taxi heading for Manhattan, passing the huge skyscrapers of New York – all concrete, steel and glass. Although she had seen the skyline from the deck of the SS *Washington*, this was different. She was now in the very heart of it, and it terrified her.

Rudolph could not resist pointing out all the 'attractions,' and plenty of others that could not even be seen from the taxi – the Bank of Manhattan Trust Building in Wall Street, '70 storeys'; the Chrysler Building, '77 storeys'; and the Empire State Building, 'tallest of all with 102 storeys, and officially the world's tallest building.'

But she was too overwhelmed by it all to take in anything he was saying. It made her feel claustrophobic. 'Oh my God! Is this where I am going to have to live?' she asked herself. It seemed unreal. How would she ever be able to adjust to this new city life?

As they drew close to the apartment block where

Rudolph had rented a room for her, Gretel saw a black man – a tall, muscular doorman standing feet astride outside an apartment block. The sight of him made her take a step backwards so that she was almost in the road. It was the first time in her life she had seen a black person.

And there was another shock awaiting her when she woke up early next morning to the roar of motor cars in the street below. Tiptoeing across to the window, she looked down to notice men urgently pouring out of apartment blocks in every direction, heading for work. How different to the view from her bedroom window in sleepy little Laupheim – the trees, green meadows and fresh clean air, a distant mountain range where she had gone skiing with her cousins.

Soon the man she loved would be joining her. They had made plans to get married and start a family. But whatever would it be like? And their children, they would have to go to school here. It made her head spin even to think of it.

As the days passed she got to know the black doorman – he came from Alabama and was not really scary at all. Soon she was smiling at him and happily asking him for directions around New York. Stop judging people by their appearance, she told herself.

But other people in uniform continued to frighten

her – even people she saw in uniforms working in cafés; they reminded her too much of the black shirts and brown shirts in Germany with their guns and whips.

* * *

Gretel's first priority in New York was to find work and earn some money. Jobs did not come easily and she knew she had to be willing to accept almost anything. It was the same for Rudolph who for a while went from door to door selling brushes.

For the first few weeks she worked as a maid to a family who had recently moved into a large apartment on West End Avenue. There she earned ten dollars a week unpacking all their belongings and moving them into their rooms. When she was no longer needed, she did a bit of cleaning and baby-sitting until she managed to get a position as a helper in a summer camp at 50 dollars for the season, with food and a room thrown in.

By the end of the summer Rudolph had got them a small apartment on the second floor of a twelve floor block at the corner of 96th Street and Broadway. Like hundreds of other families, they were shoe-horned into the dreary building. The only view from their window was a brick wall, and directly beneath them was a self-service Bickford's café, from where the deliciously sickly smell of fried food wafted into their rooms. Apart from their bedrooms, all they had was a tiny living room and a kitchenette. Still, at least they had a place of their own.

Slowly, she began to settle to her new life. At weekends and in the evenings she kept up her sport, and was offered the chance to train at the Park Central Athletic Association with Harry Wigger.

For a while she was full of self-doubts. Could it be that the Nazis had made her into such a nervous wreck that she would never be able to perform again? Wigger, who combined his role of coach with that of undertaker, was quick to reassure her, and when he praised her performance she was completely taken aback: she had almost forgotten what it was like to be valued.

All her anxieties were unfounded, and soon she began to notch up success after success. At Trenton, New Jersey, that autumn she won not just the high jump but also the shot. A huge achievement in view of her weight (she was only 51 kilograms) and her slight build.

* * *

However, it did not take long for her to realise that life in the U.S.A. was not what she had expected. She had travelled from the country where she had assumed she would be spending the rest of her life to what was supposed to be the 'Land of the Free.' But in practice she witnessed on a daily basis rampant discrimination against blacks and Jews. On trains and buses certain seats were reserved for blacks; and as for Jews, none were allowed in the golf clubs or the athletics clubs. How did the Americans have the nerve to threaten boycotting the Berlin Olympics on the grounds of Germany's racial policies when they practised many of the same policies themselves?

As often as she could she would write to Bruno, dreaming of the time when he would finish his medical training in Switzerland and they would be together again. But before that could happen she would need to raise $2,000 in sponsorship. She asked for donations for what she called her 'Bruno Fund.' Every cent she squirreled away, until eventually she had enough. The following summer the U.S. consulate granted Bruno a visa, and Gretel began to count the days until they would be together.

Perspiration dripped from her forehead as she stood on the pier at New York in the summer sun a few weeks later, awaiting Bruno's ship. She had arrived several hours before he was due, and had told her friends not to accompany her because she wanted to be on her own with Bruno.

When the ship, the SS *Rotterdam,* came into view she began to quiver, and it seemed ages before the tug boats finished pulling it in to its berth.

At last she spotted Bruno at the top of the gangplank, his eyes searching for her.

Moments later they were together, reunited at last.

Bruno would live with them in their small apartment. Since two young people of the opposite sex could not possibly move in together in those days, Rudolph offered to share his room with Bruno.

The insults soon began to fly:

'Gretel didn't say anything about your snoring when I agreed to share my room with you.'

Bruno came right back: 'I'm amazed I can get to sleep at all what with the smell of your feet.'

* * *

In Connecticut the next week she jumped 5'2" (1.57m) and won the American championship. Bruno's presence beside her was intoxicating; she felt almost weightless.

Soon they would be married. But before this could

happen they needed to save hard. Bruno took a job as a decorator, painting the ceiling of a New York hotel. Gretel continued with her summer camp job, and when it came to an end worked as a masseuse on a 'health farm' on Central Park West. Her wages would help tide her over until their wedding a few weeks later.

On 23 September Bruno and Gretel were married at City Hall, New York. With such a tight budget, the only wedding dress she could afford was black, and cost just $3. They could not run to a reception or any catering. Friends were invited to join them afterwards in a nearby restaurant – provided they paid for their own meals.

But none of this really mattered. Gretel and Bruno were on cloud nine. It was just sad that their parents could not be there on such a happy day.

She was no longer Gretel Bergmann. In the eyes of the law she was now Mrs Margaret Lambert.

Chapter 21

Following the ceremony – if something that lasted only a matter of minutes could be called one – they went on a four-day honeymoon to Atlantic City. Between them they had only $61 which they had to eke out as best they could.

When they returned from their honeymoon, Gretel went back to her job and Bruno continued his medical course. These should have been great times for the newly weds: they were together at last. Instead, their happiness was mixed with terrible anguish because of news coming out of Germany.

A Jewish lad had murdered one of the officials at the German Embassy in Paris, and in revenge the Nazis had slaughtered close on a hundred Jews in Germany. Thousands more had been arrested and sent to concentration camps. Jewish children had been dragged from orphanages, patients taken out of hospital, old people from their homes. Shops and houses owned by Jews had been looted and destroyed.

Synagogues had been burned to the ground, including the old synagogue in Laupheim. Jewish tombstones had been uprooted and graves violated. As a result of all the broken glass in the streets on the night of 9–10 November 1938, the episode quickly got the name Kristallnacht (Crystal Night).

Anxiety whether her parents and Walter were among those taken away kept Gretel awake at night. A few weeks afterwards she was in no doubt: a cryptic message from her mother said that her father was ill, and she and Walter were moving in with a widowed friend.

It was four weeks before Edwin Bergmann returned, very thin and with his hair shaved. He had been taken to the Dachau concentration camp, been given a prisoner's striped uniform and number, and made to work outside in the cold from 5 a.m. until 11 p.m. The guards had given him so little food that he now weighed only 5 stone 9 lbs (36 kgs). He was admitted to a hospital run by Catholic nuns, but as soon as the authorities found out that he was a Jew the nuns said that he must leave.

By this time the Nazis had passed a law preventing Jews from running businesses, and the Bergmann & Co. family factory had been taken over by the Nazis. Her parents were stunned: they were no longer in control of the business which had been owned by their family for generations.

They knew that they had to do everything they could to try to join Rudolph and Gretel in the U.S.A. before it was too late. It would mean leaving what little they still had behind; but that was a price well worth paying.

* * *

Just before lunch on Sunday 3 September 1939 Gretel was packing her bag ready to compete again in the American Track and Field Championships when suddenly Bruno shouted from the living room: 'Come and listen to the radio!'

England had declared war on Germany.

In tears she phoned Harry Wigger, who confirmed her fears that there would be no championship that year. Maybe she would never be able to compete again. She had dreamed of taking part in the 1940 Olympic Games as a member of the U.S. track team. But another war meant that there would be no Olympics in 1940. Even though she had moved thousands of miles away from Germany she was still being manipulated by Hitler.

Gretel felt numb, anxious about what the future

might hold for her career. By the time the 1944 Olympic Games came around she would be thirty, too old for an athlete. Even though she had moved thousands of miles away, Hitler had managed to foil her dreams once again. Her ambition was surely finally over.

Epilogue

Leaving Germany would be even harder for her parents than it had been for Gretel. Although Hitler wanted to make Germany free of Jews, those like her father who were well-off businessmen with contacts abroad, were not allowed to leave because they helped bring foreign currency into Germany. So their only option was to try leaving without all the official papers.

After a few days, the Bergmanns reached Cologne, carrying a change of clothes and their passports. In his passport her father was referred to as 'Edwin *Israel* Bergmann' and her mother as 'Paula *Sarah* Bergmann,' because of a law the Nazis had introduced so as to draw attention to Jewish heritage. Seeing as they did not have all the necessary papers to emigrate, someone must have been either very kind (or very careless) because somehow they managed to board a plane for England, from where they planned to sail to the U.S.A.

On reaching England a shock awaited them. All Jewish refugees were placed in an internment camp on the Isle of Man, alongside other citizens from hostile countries (so called 'enemy aliens') who were waiting to be summoned before the courts. No account was taken of the fact that they were fleeing from Hitler's Germany. Nor of the fact that the Bergmanns even carried visas to get them into the U.S.A. It was as if they had done something terribly wrong, as if they were criminals, just like the Nazis themselves.

From there they were taken to Liverpool. But as their ship was not ready to sail, her parents were put in jail for three days and poor Walter was sent to a Jewish family who only spoke Yiddish – a strange mixture of German and Hebrew which was not spoken by German Jews and which he did not understand.

After a journey lasting over a month, her family thankfully arrived in the U.S.A. And there was more good news because by that time Rudolph had met Ruth, the girl of his dreams, and had married her.

Her parents and Walter, who was now fourteen and becoming tall, shared an apartment with Rudolph and Ruth in 97th Street. Despite their ordeal, they adjusted well because they all spoke good English. Her father even managed to do a bit of 'hair business' again.

Now that her own family has been reunited, her

next big concern was to get Bruno's parents out of Germany. Until now they had refused even to think about leaving Andernach. Bruno's father, Simon Lambert, had fought for Germany in the Great War and he was confident of being spared arrest. But the horrors of *Kristallnacht* made them think again, and like many others, they registered with the American consulate. There they were told that due to the sheer numbers of would-be emigrants, there was little chance of getting them to the U.S.A. in the immediate future. Their only hope was to get to Cuba which was still allowing in immigrants. By means of whip-rounds and loans, Gretel managed to accumulate the necessary funds, and by November 1941 all their emigration papers were ready.

But in the following month Hitler declared war on the U.S.A. This shut off their last possible escape route, and their hopes of getting out of Germany were dashed. Soon after this, the entire Jewish population of Andernach was rounded up, put on trains and taken to concentration camps.

Meanwhile, in the U.S.A. their eldest son volunteered to serve as a doctor in the U.S. Army. His wife had planned to beat the Germans at sport, though she had never been given the opportunity she craved. Now, Bruno Lambert, proudly wearing his lieutenant's bars on his shoulders, could at last take revenge on his home country, as well as contribute something to the country that had given him a new life.

Before he could do so, he needed to get U.S. citizenship which was quickly granted because the Army needed doctors badly. The day Gretel's citizenship papers also came through had huge importance for her. She had succeeded in cutting the last link with her German past. She was no longer an 'enemy alien'; she was now the wife of an American officer.

In September 1944 Bruno's division was shipped to New York, ready to be sent to fight in Europe. As a battle surgeon, he would be working alongside the troops in the front line. Gretel, who was now pregnant, worried at the thought that her baby might never see its father.

Fortunately, the following summer Bruno safely returned, and when the war was over the couple were told to report to a hospital in Santa Fe, New Mexico. They liked the town so much that they seriously considered joining a group practice and living there. But Gretel had had two miscarriages whilst 'away from home.' She was pregnant again, and this time she wanted to have her baby back in New York. Having experienced such a bad relationship with her own mother, she desperately hoped that it would not be a daughter. Fortunately, in the following April, 1947, a son, Glenn, was born. A second son, Gary was to be born four years later.

Sadly, when Glenn was only two months old, Edwin Bergmann died suddenly of a heart attack. 'Fifteen minutes, and he was gone,' said Gretel. Although the heart attack was most probably caused by years of heavy cigar-smoking, Gretel could not help thinking that the hardships he had endured in the Dachau concentration camp had played their part.

It was a hard blow. They now had to carry on as best they could.

Bruno continued to practise medicine, making house calls and receiving frantic phone calls late at night to tend to sick children. All the while Gretel stayed at home to take care of Glenn and Gary who were growing up fast.

In 1955 the family moved to a house with a garden in the Jamaica Estates in Queen's, New York. One of their first purchases was a television, which meant that from now on they could watch every Olympic Games in comfort. Although Gretel never jumped again, she did not give up sport altogether, taking up first golf and then bowls.

As for Glenn and Gary, they moved to California, married and had families of their own. So she had to telephone them many years later, in 1980, to tell them that the German Track and Field Association had sent her a medal and had admitted her into the Jewish German Sports Hall of Fame. She wondered if they would also send her a proper letter of apology for not allowing her to participate in the Olympics. None arrived. But then, to be honest, she had not expected one.

What did arrive, sent to her by a friend, was a copy of *Time Magazine* which contained the amazing revelation that her former room-mate, Dora Ratjen, was really a man, called Hermann Ratjen! Yet, it was 'she,' not Gretel, who had been given the chance to represent Germany, even though Gretel was one of the best high jumpers in the world. Could the Nazis have known that Hermann Ratjen was a man but had still allowed him to compete in a women's event? For them, anything, rather than let a Jew take part. How she hated Germany and wanted nothing further to do with the country.

So when Gretel was invited by the German government to attend the 50th anniversary 'celebration' of the Berlin Games of 1936, she turned the invitation down without a second thought. Celebrate discrimination?

Celebrate how she had been robbed of her opportunity to win a gold medal? They had to be joking.

A celebration in her *new* country, the U.S.A., was a different matter. And when, in June 1996, she was offered the opportunity to be inducted into the U.S. National Jewish Sports Hall of Fame, she was thrilled to accept a nomination.

Immediately her story and photo appeared on the front page of the *New York Times.* She was inundated by requests for interviews the world over – from Canada to Japan, Brazil to Israel – and T.V. vans were almost permanently parked outside their house in New York.

The following month, exactly one hundred years since the modern Olympics had been introduced, the Olympic Games were held in Atlanta, Georgia. Gretel was delighted to attend as a guest of honour. And so, for the first time in her life, at the age of eighty-two, she experienced an Olympics in person.

In the autumn of 1999, she was invited to Frankfurt to receive an award. This time the decision was more difficult for her to make. She had promised herself never to set foot on German soil again but she had been nominated for the award by a friend. After wrestling with the dilemma for some days, she decided out of respect for her friend that she should go.

The very moment she agreed to accept that invitation, Gretel began to hate herself. Bruno had already made it clear that he was not prepared to go under any circumstances; he wanted to turn his back forever on his hated Germany. So she asked Glenn to accompany her to Frankfurt.

As soon as Gretel realized she was flying over German territory she began to feel awful and her heart began to pound.

Glenn held her hand.

'Why am I here?' she asked herself. 'Why am I accepting an award from those who gave me so much pain? Why did it take almost half a century for them to come forward and acknowledge the injustice done to me?' She felt angry. Nazi Germany had cheated her of the opportunity of achieving her ambition. But for a few days she would have to put these feelings aside.

When she touched down at Frankfurt airport she was given a great welcome. A delegation from Laupheim took her and Glenn to the ceremony where the mayor presented her with a cheque and a beautiful bunch of flowers. The footballer Franz Beckenbauer handed her a trophy, engraved with the words: 'To unforgotten champions.'

Glenn had for many years wanted to go to see where his father had grown up. So they took the train to Andernach and walked to the family home in Wilhelmstrasse which Gretel had visited just the once. The thought of Bruno's family being herded to the railway station and put into cattle trucks bound for unknown places was very depressing, and mother and son said very little to one another on their journey to Laupheim.

When they arrived in Gretel's home town a children's choir serenaded her with a song in Hebrew. She thought it was very sweet, even though she did not understand a word of it. After this they were taken to the gym where Gretel was given the task of unveiling a plaque carrying the words 'Gretel Bergmann Stadium.' Before they left, she showed Glenn the Bergmann factory which the Nazis had taken away from them; and the family home, barely recognizable since its conversion into a two-family house.

So Germany had at last begun to make amends. But it took another ten years until 23 November 2009, before Gretel's German national record of 1.60m from 1936 was officially restored by the German Track and Field Association. At the same time a film to celebrate her achievement, *Berlin 36,* was produced and screened in German cinemas. After so long, old wounds could now perhaps slowly begin to heal.

By sheer determination Gretel had eventually

overcome the terrible adversities that life had thrown at her. In Nazi Germany she had been shunned by her former friends, and for the safety of her family had given up the man she had planned to marry. She had been expelled from her sports club and denied a place at university. Although she was one of the best high jumpers in the world, she had been dropped from the German national team because she was a Jew. Ultimately, she had been forced to leave her native country and her family, and start a new life in a strange land.

But at the very last, justice was done, and Gretel Bergmann received her long overdue recognition.

Key dates in the life of Gretel Bergmann

1914   April 12   Born in Laupheim, Germany.

1921   Began Jewish elementary school
                        in Laupheim.

1924   Began secondary school in
                        Laupheim.

1926   Brother, Walter, is born.

1930   Spring   Enrols in an all-girls school in
                        Ulm. Joins U.F.V. sports club.

1931   Ranked fourth in Germany for
                        high jump.

1932   Ranked fifth in Germany for
                        high jump.

1933	Jan	Hitler comes to power in Germany.
		Persecution of the Jews begins.
	April	She is forced to leave her sports club for being Jewish.
		She parts from her first love, Rudi.
	Autumn	Travels to London with her father and enrols at London Polytechnic.
1934	June 30	Wins the British high jump championships at Herne Hill, London.
		She is ordered back to Germany to train for 1936 Berlin Olympics.
1935		Attends national training camp at Ettlingen.
	June	Wins the high jump championships at Ulm.
		Meets Bruno Lambert.
1936	May	She is dismissed from her sports school in Ulm.
	June 29	She equals the German high

jump record of 5' 3" (1.60m) at Stuttgart and is ranked third in the world.

July 15   U.S. Olympic team leaves for Berlin.

July 16   Gretel receives a letter, dropping her from the German team.

1937 Jan.   Her brother, Rudolph, emigrates to the U.S.A.

May 10   Gretel emigrates to the U.S.A. and settles in New York.

Sept. 25   She wins high jump and shot put at U.S. championships in Trenton, New Jersey.

1938   She again wins the U.S. high jump in Naugatuck, Connecticut.

Sept. 23   Marries Bruno Lambert in New York.

Nov.   Edwin Bergmann is taken to Dachau concentration camp.

1942   Bruno and Gretel receive United States citizenship.

		They move to Missouri, Texas and Santa Fe.
		Gretel's dear friend Rudi dies fighting as a German soldier.
1947		Returns to New York with Bruno.
	April	A son, Glenn, is born.
	June	Edwin Bergmann dies.
1951		A second son, Gary is born.
1955		She moves to New York.
1971		Her brother Rudolph dies from a heart attack while on holiday in Italy, aged 59.
1979		Paula Bergmann dies, aged 93.
1980		German Track and Field Association admits her into the Jewish German Sports Hall of Fame.
1986		She turns down an invitation to attend the 50th anniversary

celebration of the 1936 Berlin
Olympics.

1995 Aug.   A sports complex in Berlin is
named after Gretel who does not
attend the opening ceremony.

1996 June   She is inducted into the U.S.
National Jewish Sports Hall of
Fame.

July   Attends the Olympic Games at
Atlanta as guest of honour.

1999 Nov.   Returns to Germany to receive
the Georg von Opel Prize in
Frankfurt, and to open a new
sports stadium named after her
at Laupheim.

2003 June 30   Rudolph's wife, Ruth, dies, aged 87.

2009 Nov. 23   Gretel's German national record
from 1936 is officially restored
by the German Track and Field
Association.

Where to find out more

Books

Margaret Bergmann Lambert *By Leaps and Bounds* (United States Holocaust Memorial Museum, 2005)

Allen Guttman *Women's Sports. A history* (Columbia University Press, 1992)

Christopher Hilton *Hitler's Olympics* (Sutton, 2nd edn, 2008)

David Clay Large *Nazi Games. The Olympics of 1936* (W.W. Norton & Co. New York, 2007)

Robert Slater *Great Jews in Sports* (Jonathan David, New York, 2nd edn 2005) pp40-42

Films

Olympia (original footage of Berlin Olympics, 1936)

Berlin 36

Hitler's Pawn: The Margaret Lambert Story

Useful websites

http://www.youtube.com/watch?v=p_JVB42Nfok
Interview on You Tube *Holocaust Survivor
   Margaret Lambert Testimony*

http://www.youtube.com/watch?v=gNKlxcqLKcM
   The Nazi Olympics, Berlin 1936

http://www.youtube.com/watch?v=5ODX0MZgX7
   A *Jewish Athletes Part 1*

http://www.youtube.com/watch?v=kcFbVn3BeVQ
   Jewish Athletes Part 2

http://www.nydailynews.com/sports/more_sports/2
   009/11/24/2009-11-24_qns_woman_95_gets_
   olympic_record_back_after_36_nazi_team_replaced
   _her_with_man_h.html

Measures taken by the Nazis against the Jews

1933	April 1	One-day boycott of Jewish shops, lawyers and doctors all over Germany.
	April	Jews are banned from employment in the Civil Service. Thousands of Jewish bank accounts are seized.
	May 26	Public burning of books by Jewish authors.
	Sept.	Jews are banned from owning farms.
1935	Spring	In Munich the S.A. sprays racist graffiti on Jewish shops and assaults Jews in the streets in broad daylight.
	May	Jews are forbidden to join the army.
	June 13-19	Nazis attack Jews and 'Jewish-

looking' people in Kurfürstendamm Street, Berlin, smashing women in the face.

Sept. 15 *The Nuremberg Laws* ban marriages between Jews and Aryans, and forbid them to have sexual relations outside marriage.

1936 March 7 Jews can no longer vote.

 July The anti-Jewish campaign is suspended while the Olympic Games are taking place in Berlin. Anti-Jewish signs are taken down.

 Dec. 21 Jewish doctors in Germany are forced to resign their posts in private hospitals.

1937 Sept. Hitler makes an outspoken attack on the Jews. More Jewish businesses are confiscated.

1938 April Jews have to register their property, making it easier to confiscate.

June-July	Jewish doctors, dentists and lawyers are forbidden to treat Aryans.
July 17	All Jews have to add either 'Israel' or 'Sarah' to their name.
July 27	All 'Jewish' street names are to be replaced.
Oct.	Jews must have a red letter 'J' stamped on their passports.
Nov. 9-10	Kristallnacht (Crystal Night). Nazis destroy synagogues, Jewish homes and shops.
Nov. 12	Nazis fine the Jews one billion Reichmarks for the damage.
Nov. 15	Jews are excluded from schools, universities, cinemas and sports facilities.
Nov. 23	All Jewish businesses are closed down and taken over by the Nazis.
1939 Jan.	Reich office for Jewish Emigration is established to promote emigration 'by every possible means.'
Sept. 23	All Jews must hand their radios

in to the police.

1940	July 29	Jews are no longer allowed to have telephones.
1941	Sept. 1	Every Jew in Germany over six years old has to wear a yellow star of David in public.
	Oct. 15	Jews are forbidden to keep dogs, cats and birds.
1942	Jan.	Jews are banned from all public baths.
	Feb.	Jews are forbidden to buy firewood, newspapers and magazines.
	May	Jews are banned from many areas of Berlin.
	June	Jews have to surrender their cameras to the government.
	July 17	Blind or deaf Jews are no longer allowed to wear armbands identifying their condition in traffic.

Summer Olympic Games Sites
in modern times

Between 776 B.C. and 393 A.D. the Games were held every four years in the Greek city of Olympia. The different city states of Greece competed, and only men were allowed to enter.

The Olympics were revived by Baron Pierre de Coubertin in 1896. He enthusiastically supported the Games, believing they would encourage healthy competition between athletes, and have a role in promoting peace and understanding across cultures.

Athens, Greece	1896
Paris, France	1900
St Louis, U.S.A.	1904
London, U.K.	1908
Stockholm, Sweden	1912
Scheduled for Berlin, Germany	1916
Antwerp, Belgium	1920

Paris, France	1924
Amsterdam, Netherlands	1928
Los Angeles, U.S.A.	1932
Berlin, Germany	1936
Scheduled for Tokyo, Japan	1940
Scheduled for London, U.K.	1944
London, U.K.	1948
Helsinki, Finland	1952
Melbourne, Australia	1956
Rome, Italy	1960
Tokyo, Japan	1964
Mexico City, Mexico	1968
Munich, Germany	1972
Montreal, Canada	1976
Moscow, Russia	1980
Los Angeles, U.S.A.	1984
Seoul, South Korea	1988
Barcelona, Spain	1992
Atlanta, U.S.A.	1996
Sydney, Australia	2000
Athens, Greece	2004
Beijing, China	2008
London, U.K.	2012
Scheduled for Rio de Janeiro, Brazil	2016

MIND GAMES

Can YOU clear the bar? Set the bar at 1.51m and try to work your way up!

1.60 Which concentration camp was Gretel's father taken to?

1.59 What nationality was the woman who won gold in the high jump at Berlin?

1.58 Where was the main German national training camp?

1.57 Where was the British Amateur Athletics Association competition in 1934?

1.56 How much money was Gretel allowed to take to the U.S.A.?

1.55 Who was Gretel's room-mate who turned out to be a man?

1.54 What was the name of Gretel's lover from whom she was forced to part?

1.53 What was the name of Hitler's 'master race?'

1.52 What used to be grown on her training ground in Laupheim?

1.51 In which country was Gretel Bergmann born?

Annoying Anagrams

but have a go anyway!

WIN BRONZE

for
MINI TEAM SITS
(Clue: discrimination against Jews)

WIN SILVER

for
COMELY RIPCORD
(Clue: Gretel's dream)

WIN GOLD

for
BARON TUMBLER
(Clue: Precious U.S. import!)

Crossword

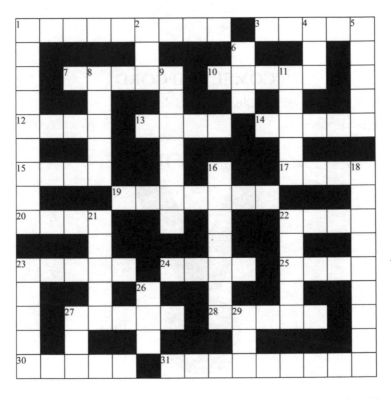

Frame by FT

Clues Across

1 Olympic event often involving swimming, cycling and running (9)

3 Leap over object using a long pole (5)

7 Spectators (5)

10 Gretel slipped to this position in the high jump after she met Rudi (5)

12 The ____ put was another of Gretel's skills (4)

13 Metal used to make the first place medal (4)

14 Young Rudolph and Gretel played one on their piano teacher (5)

15 The Jews ____ the Nazis one billion Marks after Kristallnacht (4)

17 ____ strait leads to the finishing line (4)

19 Arena where many games take place (7)

20 ____ Jackson finished fourth for England in 800m at Commonwealth Games 2010 (4)

22 In 1936 Germany was the ____ for the Olympic Games (4)

23 The Olympic flag has five of these (5)

24 Union Jack, for example (4)

25 It transported Gretel and her father from Herne Hill stadium to the railway station (4)

27 What competitors do in a velodrome (5)

28 Soaring bird on German coat of arms (5)

30 None of Gretel's family were in the slightest bit interested in it (5)

31 Frenchman who revived Ancient Olympics (9)

Clues Down

1 One of those uprooted during Kristallnacht (9)

2 Trainers show athletes ____ (3)

4 Exclamation of disgust (3)

5 ____ and field (5)

6 What every athlete is determined to do! (3)

8 Odam of England was highly ____ (5)

9 The black one Gretel saw in New York startled her (7)

11 This holds the Olympic flame (5)

16 Where the male Olympic athletes lived (7)

18 Site of big national training camp in Germany (9)

21 Gretel's mood when she opened the letter from Tschammer (5)

22 Where her father stayed on his business trip to London (5)

23 Those leading to the Reich Stadium were widened (5)

26 To escape to England Gretel's family knew they would have to do this from Cologne (3)

27 Sound made by 20,000 Olympic pigeons (3)

29 At last, in May 1937 Gretel sailed into New York h____our (3)

Answers

Can YOU clear the bar?

1.51 Germany

1.52 Potatoes

1.53 Aryan

1.54 Rudi

1.55 Dora Ratjen

1.56 $4

1.57 Herne Hill, south London

1.58 Ettlingen

1.59 Hungarian

1.60 Dachau

Annoying Anagrams
Bronze: Antisemitism
Silver: Olympic record
Gold: Bruno Lambert

Crossword

Clues Across	**Clues Down**

Clues Across

1   Triathlon
3   Vault
7   Crowd
10 Fifth
12 Shot
13 Gold
14 Trick *or* Prank
15 Owed
17 Home
19 Stadium
20 Emma
22 Host
23 Rings
24 Flag
25 Taxi
27 Cycle
28 Eagle
30 Sport
31 Coubertin

Clues Down

1   Tombstone
2   How
4   Ugh
5   Track
6   Win
8   Rated
9   Doorman
11 Torch
16 Village
18 Ettlingen
21 Angry
22 Hotel
23 Roads
26 Fly
27 Coo
29 Arb

ACKNOWLEDGEMENTS

I would like to thank my brother, Brian, for suggesting that I write this book. Kara Gibbs kindly shared her expertise at high jumping and provided me with very useful information about training. I also wish to thank Mollie Cheek, Isobel Cook, Lydia Crosher, Rebecca Epps, Christie-Jade Mallett, Diana Williams and Sophie Woodin for reading and commenting on earlier drafts of this book.